LIQUIDATING PERRY

A Novella

ZACHARY AMENDT

Underground Voices
Los Angeles, California
2016

Published by Underground Voices
www.undergroundvoices.com
Editor contact: Cetywa Powell

ISBN: 978-0692690574

Printed in the United States of America.

© 2016 by Zachary Amendt. All rights reserved.

TABLE OF CONTENTS

Chapter One   5
Peep

Chapter Two   21
Berdoo

Chapter Three   42
Reagan and Spock

Chapter Four   66
Advertisements of Himself

Chapter Five   87
Uphill Two Bottles with Four Miles of Wine

Chapter Six   118
The Saint's Blood Liquefies

Chapter Seven   133
Patrón Saint

In Peril of Death   144

About the Author   149

Chapter One - Peep

It was a life of seven milestones. Seven sacraments. Although I think Perry would disagree.

But he's not here to.

In the end, it was easier for him to sell his soul than to save it.

He drank. Alcohol was his vitamin. It was his two-a-day, his downfall.

The only wagon he thought much of was *The War Wagon*, the western, that one with John Wayne.

Liquidating Perry

Peep.
  His siblings didn't call him Perry. They called him

  We didn't call him Dad. He was Perry to us.
  Technically Perry was a deadbeat, but deadbeat is often too reductive, too easy and all-encompassing. Deadbeat didn't fit Perry. It's not as though he forgot his children – he was just incapable of putting himself second.
  It wasn't personal. It was just all about him.
  Perry first. Perry to the lifeboats.

Liquidating Perry

His PIN was the last four digits of his SSN. He was a Baby Boomer, unwittingly ripe for fraud. When he needed something – a job, a place to stay – he consulted the classified pages, where nothing exists anymore. That is, until he learned how to use 'the computer.' He kept all technology in the lower case – i.e., tv, internet. They were not proper nouns to him, but effronteries.

His was a working retirement. He had no pension. Substitute teaching did not supplement his income; it was his only income. This was 2007. He was drinking Michelob, which he dubbed his *teacher juice*. His kindergartners would have to wake him up after nap-time.

Fatigue – of drinking and of life – doesn't set in as much as it moves in. What made Perry different was his decline, how he embraced it and made it into a kind of artform. What set him apart was how he died, on the upswing, after decades of backsliding, drink and homelessness.

His death was tragic. The outcome is not tragic.

I distrust my memory. I'm sure I've distorted it and so it's at times a polluted thing, full of wastrel, clogged by dregs.

This is the book I had no plans to write. This book is the flotsam. It's what was findable about Perry. It's what I could salvage of him.

Writing this is like having him as a parent all over again, for the very first time.

As for what isn't in here, it must be so traumatic that it's worth suppressing.

My brother Travis objects to this, every word of it. Not the actual text or the truth of it, but the principle. Perry wasn't these things to both of us. He wasn't so mythic to my brother. He could really be quite mean.

Liquidating Perry

To what end? Perry often asked, of nearly everything. *To what end?*

It was his rubric, his litmus test. He thought everyone should have their own rhetorical question.

He had other catch phrases.

This could be the night, he said, almost every night. Individually the nights matter. Collectively they're nothing. When I told him when he was in hospice that he was dying (all those nights, all that drink), that the cancer had moved to his liver, he offered me a Kleenex because he could see me crying through my aviators.

I said his kidneys were failing, had failed.

He did not believe me. He was still flirting with the hospital staffers changing out his bedpan.

I'm dying, he asked.

Yes, I said. Don't blame the nurses. It wasn't their place to tell you.

And later, out of intensive care, when his nerves were singing – *the worst pain of my life, you have no idea, Zachary, how much pain* – when he gently asked if I had maybe, inadvertently, signed away his right to painkillers.

I still shudder.

Life support it turns out isn't one thing, one plug or one intervention. It's a dozen things: air tubes, monitors, morphine.

I feel safe with you, were probably not Perry's last words. But they were the last ones of his I heard.

Liquidating Perry

I was living in New York at the beginning of Perry's infirmity. He thought there were six boroughs. He wanted to know where the Big Apple was, on what intersection. And how big was it, really? Two stories high? Taller?

He might not have been joking.

Perry did rally for a few years, toward the end. He got sober. He focused on his health. He had a roof over his head, finally.

I believe he wanted grandchildren, very badly, but he only asked once.

As a favor, he said.

It is as strange outliving one's parents as the reverse. I feel what Sofia Tolstoy felt, as she reflected on hers and Lev's romance: It is cruel that life can end in anything except more life.

My great-grandfather was 99 when he slipped the proverbial surly bonds. My grandfather 79. Perry 59.

I'm 31.

I will end this trend.

Liquidating Perry

Knowing our family history brings little comfort. It disheartens me to see all the errors repeated, the prophets spurned. My past prepares me for what's to come, for the day when I repeat it, all of it, and do it all bigger – especially the mistakes.

I pressed Perry once about my past. He was not forthcoming but I insisted on an answer. What was I like as a child, I wanted to know.

You didn't cry much, was all he said. *You liked bread.*

Italics, because it was always Perry's emphasis. Never ours.

Liquidating Perry

Perry's story means there's some user assembly required. He cannot remain unknown. He should have known I wouldn't have let him off that easy.

I'm not sanitizing him. You see his tarnish, his rust. I'm trying to get an idea of the scale of his intricacies, his peccadilloes. I'm trying to figure out whether or not he was objectively fascinating, or if he is just because I say he is.

In many ways this is the man I wanted my father to be. It's more than entertainment or amusement. It's a meditation on how to deal.

A relationship is like anything. You have to talk about it to make it work. If I talk about Perry, he still matters. Using the present tense is important because he's alive in these pages, in-between the covers, where he always felt safest.

He put so little of himself down on paper. Documents as simple as a resume were a tough nut for him to crack. He didn't fully list his accomplishments. He had forgotten many of them. Like his college transcripts, they were all so old, old enough for microfilm.

Liquidating Perry

It is not a linear life and it can't be one compiled of strictly fact.

Perry was influenced by God, then Marlboro, then Ford, then Smirnoff.

He was not drafted during Vietnam.

In the end, he was less important to his nation than he was to its distilleries.

Liquidating Perry

There were hard, unmentionable, latchkey years.

People get stuck on barstools, glued. Perry was stuck. He drowned his sorrows, and his sorrows were not shallow, or easily drowned.

The biggest struggle is not to fall into his traps, given how adept he was at self-destruction. He wasn't a great father or husband and I'm not sure if he ever bothered trying to be at minimum a good one. The point of this isn't to exonerate him as much as I want to figure him out, and in doing so figure myself out, because I'm his next genetic approximation. I have his hunger, his thirst.

But this isn't about my drinking. It's about his.

Court documents are a veritable treasure trove of Perry. Lawsuits, affidavits. He was cynical about weddings, but not about marriages. He remarried in 1992 because he thought we needed a female figure, someone maternal, a stand-in for our real mother who, on an innocuous Tuesday late in 1985 while Perry was out-of-town for an oil conference, packed a suitcase and left us with some toys in the crib we shared.

Two days later he found us, more worse-for-wear than I want to admit.

She was gone. There were no charges to press.

I don't call her Mom. Her name is Kathleen – which, because she's still alive, is not her name either.

Divorcing Perry was a formality. She might as well have listed Travis and I as respondents.

A diaper, after all, is a euphemism for something you don't want to do, or change.

Perry blamed himself for her leaving. He never stopped blaming himself. He never disparaged her. He even sang her praises, making up new ones along the way.

Our loved ones deserve documentaries. The book is not always better than the movie.

If only someone could have run a PSA of Perry's life in 1978. That year he was handed the reins of the family oil business, a Texaco affiliate. He was 25 years old and dating the prettiest girl at Riverside High School.

Kathleen. She was 16.

Those were different times, years of strange permissions.

I suspect physical intimacy was something Perry did not enjoy so much as regret afterward. There were penalties attached to it, such as VD, children. Us.

Liquidating Perry

This isn't a *my-father-was-an-alcoholic-woe-is-me*. I refuse to even associate the word with him. No-one had taught him providence, not that he'd have listened. Still, after work he'd pour his first enormous glass of absinthe, which would become cloudy after an hour, lukewarm.

At least once a week he spilled it on our dog.

One needn't drink for enjoyment. There are sundry other amusements. It inclines you to shut yourself in, but not so with Perry. Drinking shut him out. He was particular about what he did and didn't drink in the house. Gin, for example. He never kept gin at home.

At least, not in plain view.

Or, in any of the hiding spots we could think of.

Because he loved it that much.

I asked him what it was like to spend so much time in bars. I meant to disprove him.

Be prepared to talk baseball, he said. *And to see grown men cry. All day.*

He would disagree with these milestones. He'd add to them. *The day a gallon of fuel cost one dollar,* he'd say. *The day Liston knocked out Patterson,* he'd say.

I've done the math. I've traced his steps. Perry's was a plotless life.

My autocorrect function just changed 'plotless' to 'pointless.'

I'm afraid much of this amounts to a false nostalgia, when I really wish to retire my nostalgia, to table it indefinitely. I never thought that I would have these words or know what to do with them. But Perry wouldn't want it sugarcoated.

His aging was fascinating and premature. As were his multiple homelessnesses. It was riches-to-rags. Necessities became luxuries. He had taken to sitting in the dark, walking with his head down. He told us that if he collapsed, if he fell apart, it was an inside job. That it was only him who could scuttle his life.

Yet even at his nadir and lowest ebb I didn't pity him, not once. Pity is the worst to feel for someone, because it's not for them. It's for you.

It was cancer, ultimately. Cancer takes the mystery out of life. And yet, a life ending is different from a life being over. Nothing about Perry is contingent on times or years and it is only urgent in so far as I'm leaking memories of him like a sieve, or a faulty radiator, until one day I'll empty of Perry.

Every day I try to remember something new about him.

Thirty-one. Days with my genes are not plentiful.

Chapter Two – Berdoo

Perry's past is better plumbed, not excavated. He needs unearthing without inventory. Any comprehension of him belongs with the shards, the bones.

Still, it wouldn't hurt to know where we are. This is a family history. Location matters.

In the 1940s San Bernardino was renowned for its rampant prostitution and as a watering hole for the stars. 'Berdoo' was also the last stop on the long drive to Las Vegas.

In most other towns the heights were where the affluence was. Not there.

It's your hometown, Perry would say later. *It's always yours.*

Berdoo was far from the terrestrial paradise. Sammy Davis, Jr. lost his right eye in a car accident on Cajon Boulevard and Kendall Drive. Gene Hackman was born there. So too was Perry Steven Amendt on January 27, 1953, to Leo and Eloise Amendt.

Who we did not call Grandpa and Grandma, but Leo and Eloise.

Not all beginnings are humble. He was very much a Perry, after Perry Como, the crooner. It's not the commonest of names. He was the Amendts' third child, the offspring of the American Dream. Like all children Perry had untold abilities, inexhaustible possibilities. His future failures were a glimmer in no-one's eyes in the Eisenhower era, where Berdoo was like milk and honey.

For Leo, a city's wildlife was its people. It was a question not of the size of the fish but the volume of the pond. He was big deal in the Inland Empire. He founded an oil company and a bank and ran for city council. It was an era of slogans ('*Rinse and repeat*,' '*Guinness is good for you*') and hot-rods and grooming Richard Nixon for President. Deals were closed on a handshake. It was easier to renege on promises in those days, harder to sue. Unscrupulous people love handshake deals. They're easy to fake. All you have to do is squeeze.

Liquidating Perry

We're all a part of history, even if we don't want to be.

Here's Leo's fame: until Gov. Gray Davis, he was the last politician in California to be successfully recalled from office.

Even dubious honors are honors nonetheless.

Parents play favorites. As they should. As Leo did.

Adversity did not build up Perry's character. It built callouses.

Perry was the younger sibling with something to prove. He was not much of a student. He found the chalkboard to be like a minefield, an illegible mess. In class he asked too many questions, the wrong ones. He asked the nuns at Aquinas High School *why* when he should have just responded *yes, sister*.

After years of such indoctrination he came to believe in God, not the God in the machine – *deux ex machina* – but the genderless, vengeful God.

This was the teenage Perry. For the adult Perry, there was no God. There was only Murphy's Law.

San Bernardino is the town you move to when you're in the Witness Protection Program.

Perry's closest culture growing up was television. His second closest culture was Los Angeles.

He went to his junior and senior dances with Debbie Huntsman. He was in braces and in love. He came to believe in himself through her and through sports, just as I've found him in clippings from the sports pages Eloise scrapbooked:

> The Aquinas Falcons bombed the Sherman Indians 8-3 in an afternoon game, April 2, [1971]. The big gun in the Aquinas arsenal was Perry Amendt, Aquinas' second baseman. Amendt parked two pitches into the street in the slugfest. It is the first time someone has driven out two homers in a long time; also played superbly with the glove.

Talent isn't supposed to stay raw. One's abilities are supposed to ripen. Perry was stocky like a second baseman and just as selfish, wanting to be in on every play, every pitch. He also excelled at basketball, enamored of the squeaky shoes, the gleaming hardwood.

They were not always winning teams. Losing was meant to be handled casually, effervescently. One had to be as magnanimous in defeat as in victory.

If you can't win, then lose the biggest, he often reminded us.

At 18 Perry was like wine. He may not have known it, but he was. He needed TLC, to be served at a slight chill. After twenty years he would peak.

He graduated Aquinas in '71 and enrolled in California State University, San Bernardino, which he anointed "the Dartmouth of the West Coast."

Choosing colleges is akin to choosing five or six mutually exclusive futures. As Clark Kerr once put it, universities exist chiefly "to provide sex for students, sports for alumni, and parking for faculty." CSUSB was a college not for substandard students but for locals in need of a trade. A commuter school, perfect for Perry. He was smart in an arty way – which is to say not smart, but sensitive. A critical thinker but not a genius. Not bookish but collegiate. His long curly hair suggested intensity and creativity, but the truth was that he couldn't sit still long enough for a haircut.

It's the laughter down the hall you envy, the classes that let out early, the minds that are blissfully disengaged. Fraternity parties were not confined to houses off-campus. Berdoo was a military and steel town. Every day was a frat party. The sororities, in contrast, were convents.

His college papers and lecture notes are rare glimpses into his learning, like a love letter to his old self, like a recipe book one makes before learning about dietary restrictions. His handwriting was clear and even and legible, and this is another thing that skips generations.

I find I need a decoder ring for my own handwriting.

And like Perry I work slow, in longhand. I work so slow, sloths laugh at me.

He thought he was his teachers' peer, their equal, as if his professors hadn't earned their patches. Too congenial for the academics' liking. Too independent. He didn't ask for advice or help, which they, being mentors, resented.

It wasn't ego. He just didn't want to be a nuisance. He didn't want to bother.

Drinking is no help to the Amendts. It seems to mute our brilliance.

Leo sold Ancient Age, a true swill of a bourbon, before he opened Amendt Oil Company. He was grooming Perry to take it over one day. This was not cheating – it was nepotism.

Work that defines a man defiles him. Amendt Oil was a Texaco distributorship and Perry was on call 24/7. Automation was supposed to reduce work hours, not increase them, but the system Leo pioneered to manage the oil business – the Card-Gard – was constantly breaking down.

In college Perry had studied the anthropology of philosophy, not computers. He was proud of the hours he spent repairing the faulty machines. He wanted to share this new proficiency of his with Leo, who had been so proud of Perry when he was the baseball star, the favored prospect. But Leo didn't want to know how the machines ran. It was like a car engine. There was no artistry to speak of. He wanted them to run. That was all.

This was a man who, after he was deputized as an honorary county Sheriff, tried to carry a revolver onto a plane.

I mean Leo, naturally. Perry was just a little more by the book.

Liquidating Perry

There's a Jerome Kern verse that cites Perry as a young man.

> Who cares if my boat goes upstream,
> Or if the gale bids me go with the river's flow?
> I drift along with my fancy.
> Sometimes I thank my lucky stars my heart is free.
> And other times I wonder, where's the mate for me?

Perry was not a product of his generation – he was *the* product. The consummate unprofessional. It didn't matter who was getting married, or who had died, because like the Levi's executives, Perry wore jeans. He preferred duds, denim. He felt most uncomfortable in suits, most insecure in clothes that fit him quite well.

His pockets were his briefcase. He folded contracts in half. He doodled on leases.

He didn't have to try to make friends. He made them immediately, like instant potatoes. Just add water, or in his case, whiskey.

He spent on vacations, not properties.

He spent on alcohols, not clothes.

Fun was non-negotiable to him. He was fit and his body rejoiced after an enervating run through Arrowhead Golf Course, followed by twenty pushups and a Jack LaLaine smoothie. He had a yen for the good life because the good life kept getting better. If he found out a friend was pregnant he issued condolences instead of congratulations. Otherwise he was the nice young man with the hipflask and the good last name.

Until he got into trouble.

Trouble is what we all have in common.

At 25 Perry was still coy about women, covert. Leo had taught him to drive defensively and fall in love defensively. Women were not a trifle to him. Damsels were never not in distress.

Liquidating Perry

What his heart needed wasn't a woman, I think, but a night watchman.

Liquidating Perry

I'm told that Kathleen played hard-to-get. I'm uncertain how they were introduced. Perry claimed that she pulled up to one of Amendt Oil's fueling islands in a blood-red MG and that he bolted from his second-floor office to get her number.

He said it was like she was juggling sunlight. It beamed from her, her aura, her limbs.

He said he didn't know she was sixteen. She didn't look sixteen, he said. She had none of a sixteen-year-old's inhibition.

Eventually, though, he knew, and it didn't deter him.

Kathleen was like catnip to him. She played hard to get. Resistance was the key to gaining muscle and it was also the secret to keeping Perry interested. He said that despite her cotillion training she had a sailor's mouth and a sportswriter's humor. She laughed at Monty Python. She was not offended by Benny Hill.

Today the only sense I can make of it all is by piecemeal, by slumming and delving. By hearsay. I know that when Kathleen graduated high school she moved in with Perry. He had bought a house on D St, in the (then) toniest part of town. I imagine, driving by it now, that what the house needed for them to succeed as a couple was a red front door. That a red door would ward off any domestic trouble. I picture Kathleen painting it red, ruining her favorite jeans, and wallpapering the foyer with reams of flowers that would never die. I imagine a quiet life where any noise – jazz music, the lawnmower – was an interloper. I see Perry skimming through recipes, seeking inspiration. (After all, the best way to end traditional gender roles is to get half of them wrong.) After dinner, Kathleen pours him a nightcap. Later he teaches her how to mix cocktails, and soon she's bartending for him, as long as the drinks don't get more complicated than a martini.

What I mean is that I see them happy. I must.

You never saw two people so happy, Kathleen's mother once told me. *At least, in public.*

She turned 18. The piano was calling her name, as was the harp, as was Berkeley, as was the Peace Corps. She had movie-star looks – she won an Olivia Newton-John lookalike contest in 1980 – but it doesn't matter who you look like, because eventually you'll look like an older version of that person.

It is not being a fly on the wall during the events leading up to your conception as much as believing that both parties' hearts were in it. In 1981 she gets pregnant. Perry obliges her to get an abortion, and the next year, a second one.

He wasn't ready for children. He didn't want them to interrupt his fun. But she was ready, and she hid her third pregnancy from him.

Me.

I am third.

That's why she's so thin in her wedding pictures.

As if, after two abortions, they needed another reason to stay together.

Perry reminded me that I wasn't wanted. He often called me a broken condom.

It sucks when you're the part of someone's life that they'd do over. I must have sensed his reticence.

You didn't kick in the womb, he later said. *You punched.*

The big rumor I grew up with was that in her second trimester he drove Kathleen to Palm Springs, where the middleweights used to train before big boxing bouts. The Amendt name had some cache then, enough to get him behind the scenes, backstage, where he jumped rope with Roberto Duran and asked 'Marvelous' Marvin Hagler to autograph Kathleen's stomach.

Marvelous obliged.

Liquidating Perry

February of 1983 was three months before I was born. At six months in the womb the skin is still translucent. I was developing my first emotions. My eyes were turning blue.

It was very much a 1983 wedding. Kathleen wore a hat. Perry's suit and his limousine matched, a nauseating brown.

I don't know where they honeymooned. Even if I wanted to know, I'm not sure who to ask.

Marriage is like a quiz show. I think I know the answer, but I don't. But I buzz in anyway. They were not happy together – they slept on opposite sides of the house for thirty years – and yet my wife and I honeymooned where Leo and Eloise honeymooned, at the Hotel Del Coronado. For the life of me I'm not sure why I was so insistent on retracing the beginning steps of such a dissolute marriage.

I know why, my wife said. You're nostalgic for all the wrong things. Like cowboys and Indians. Nostalgic for things you never knew.

What astonishes me is that – knowing about Perry and Leo and all my predilections – she still wants to have children with me.

She also asks, when we go on vacation or out on the town, why I feel the need to be so idiosyncratic, to lead as large a life as I can, as if it was Perry's fault in any way.

Which, of course, it is.

Liquidating Perry

I was born, like Samuel Beckett, on a Friday the 13th.

Beckett and I own all of the superstitions.

During his rehearsal dinner speech the night before our wedding in 2010, Perry said that May 13, 1983, was not only a Friday, but also a full moon.

My father-in-law, during his speech, corrected Perry. There was no moon, he said.

Liquidating Perry

Perry called Kathleen *the mistress of invisible distances*. Photographs (and Travis) are all I have of them together. She was pretty. She spent his money like she hated it. In this way they were not only eerily similar but kindred. They were young and free to do anything, and so they did nothing, traveled nowhere, except once, on a packet tour of Europe (it was not *Parisiennes* to Perry, but *Parisites*) taking abominable Polaroids, acting like insufferable Americans. There's one picture of them – it's warping and yellowing from age – at the Leaning Tower of Pisa with other tourists queued up to mime propping it up. Perry's hand is at 8 degrees; the tower is at 6. She's in a sundress. They're smiling.

Italy, and the price of film. You have to smile.

Liquidating Perry

Memories are constellations and they are also archipelagos. If I was a rock climber I would say they were foot-holds, and if I were an orphan I would say they were figments, fakes.

My mother's innocence was not something for her to maintain but to vacate.

As if you can abdicate from motherhood, which apparently you can.

At thirty-one, I still don't know how to spend Father's Day or Mother's Day. I feel not unlike that scene from *Father of the Bride* where Spencer Tracy tries on his wedding suit and he's so proud that he fits in it but he really doesn't.

What I mean is, I can shatter a lot. I can fall to pieces. But I have to be the glue of my family and at the same time, my own glue.

I'm not painting Perry in the best light but in a good enough light, one that won't burn out on him. Having a child, it turned out, meant more drinking for him, not less. Chips on the shoulder were to be knocked off, but Perry's seemed cemented on. He got more peppery in the temples. His beard was less auburn and fiery. Amendt Oil soldiered on. The sounds of industry are not home sounds but commercial sounds, a cacophony of money. Work was a maelstrom of deadlines, but it was not *all* work. He would play touch football with lawyers and accountants after work in the parking lot of Court Street West – his favorite bar – suits versus skins. When he drank with them it was vitriol, it was tearing off his t-shirts *a la* Hulk Hogan. He turned into Prince Charming at midnight and the pumpkins became glass slippers.

It wasn't delirium tremens, but delirium tremendous.

His twenties were the autobiography of a generation. It was slapdash, unrelenting movement. Drinks came on like a blitzkrieg, in waves.

His twenties were like the American autobahn. He uncorked it. All speed, no rules.

At this point in Perry's life I'd have been seven months old and Kathleen would have known she was pregnant a fourth time with what would be her second child.

Like Perry, like thoroughbreds. He doesn't want to win, but to run, eat oats, go to stud.

Deviousness was Robert Mitchum's prescription for a healthy marriage, but I think if my parents had shared a megalomania-in-tandem that they might have worked out their problems.

Parenting is just like a horror flick. It's a terrible idea to split up. But it was the point where they became clumsy around one another. The marriage was snowmelt, suddenly. They started keeping different hours. They stopped making meals together.

Liquidating Perry

Family law's a great industry, Perry said in 1996, holding the remit envelope for his alimony. *It's recession proof.*

I don't know why Kathleen left. I imagine, if I asked Perry today, he'd shrug. Better to evade, admit nothing. Deny everything. Demand proof.

If she was ever ugly to me it's because I incited her toward it, he said later. *If she was ever mean to me it's because I was mean first.*

There are only two sides to their story together, and this is the chief problem with not just memory, but also with the judicial system.

Divorce was Perry's first milestone: Evidence of What He Could Not Get Away With. He had a talent for alienating loved ones. He promised a lot and delivered slowly on his promises. But he was capable of unabashedly sweet gestures. I know, because at bedtime he would mix his martinis and kamikazes in the bathroom, just so as not to wake us.

Liquidating Perry

There's no playbook for a good relationship, except all of literature and nearly every film. I would not characterize them as bad for each other, simply wrong for each other. They were married two years. It's like a cold case, an unsolvable crime. I don't want to dredge it all up. The dust that's settled shouldn't be disturbed.

Setbacks, Perry said. *Ignore. Move on.*

Kathleen's leaving was his first homelessness. He did what we would have done today but he was the first of the divorcees to do it: he moved back in with Leo and Eloise.

They were free rent, free babysitting to him. A trampoline. A safety net.

Perry wasn't child-centric, and 1985 wasn't a time where the parental wellness orbited around the kids. His routine revolved around the bottle. A drink at the end of the day was not a reward for a hard day's work, but a primer. Whiskey made him lovely, affectionate. Sundays were not for the Sabbath, but – given the options on the jukeboxes in Berdoo's dive bars – Black Sabbath.

He partied. He stayed out until dawn.

People look amazing in candlelight, he said, *and in strobe light.*

But moving back home was like hitting the reset button on all of that.

My trouble is not being motherless, but mentorless.

Perry was Perry was Perry and he was irrevocably him and at times he was more of himself than other times, and when he was himself he was a king. But it's hard for me to herald his complexity when the logic behind his decision making – he didn't make decisions in as much as he made reactions, knee-jerk ones – was convoluted or non-existent.

Then again, the hardest thing is for the king to ask for help. Help was a crutch, and you went to places like home (and Lourdes) to get rid of your infirmity.

We had no family traditions, just the one family car, the one pet, the one parent. And then we were all under one roof, three generations, for three years. And whatever Perry did at the office – the rare times he closed an account himself – did not exonerate or exempt him from chores.

Liquidating Perry

Drinking doesn't run in our family. It gallops.
No one is more worried about my drinking than I am ... was Perry's way of preempting any intervention.

He drank as if it was the occupational hazard of single parents. For all the good it did for his stress-levels and social life, the consequences crept up on him.

Impotence is one, he claimed.

The lucky drinkers have watershed quitting moments like DUIs. The unlucky ones have nothing to stop it from slowly renting them asunder.

In his effects with his report cards and Prom photos I came across a note the teenage Perry had left for Leo, who in the 1960s would also leave at night in hot pursuit of the same thrills Perry later sought.

I'm tired of you going out and leaving Mom and I until midnight wondering.
You promised.
You swore not to 'cut back.' You swore to quit.

Which were words Perry would not eat later because I didn't shove them down his throat.

Although I should have.

Chapter Three – Reagan and Spock

Childhood was not many things. It was not right, not ideal, not boring.

My father was a great teacher, Charles Bukowski said about his. *He taught me the meaning of pain. Pain without reason.*

We were unplanned and unwanted. Eventually Perry came to stop resenting us for truncating his youth.

He led a double life, a triple life. Father. Oil executive. Barfly.

He was a single parent, not a superhero. He was not a man of steel. He was, by his own admission, a man of steel wool.

Some days I think he was a bad man but a good father. Some days it's vice versa.

He was the paragon of curiosity. He had friends, not hobbies. He had flings, not loves. But he stepped up. He fathered. Despite his nominal business acumen, he saved and bought his dream home on 615 W. 34th, a mortgage that came with furniture and wind chimes and bird feeders made from Popsicle sticks.

I say 'Perry' when I should be saying 'Dad.'

Dad and Perry were not synonymous, nor interchangeable.

Never 'Dad.' It was as if Perry was allergic to palindromes and honorifics.

It was 1988. Perry enrolled us into a school with a uniform policy because children are as cruel as adults when it comes to clothing. In Catholic School you learn that oppressive leadership is supposed to be good for you. That tyrants have hearts. I was old at 5, an old man, a pre-school geriatric. I did not share. I did not know how to draw between the lines. I was a white kid from the suburbs, a dime-a-dozen. I was a child but not childish. Whatever the weather was, was also my mood.

Liquidating Perry

My childhood was not a Norman Rockwell or Thomas Kincade painting. It was a Pollack piece, a Warhol. I was raised on fault lines, on shaky San Andreas ground. There was no critical language for Perry's parenting. He parented on abbreviated hours. His parenting was *laissez-faire*, hands off. He didn't obsess over the hardwood being scratched up, or tears in the sofa, or crayon on the walls. Objects were perishables, and nothing was made to stay pristine. A glass was meant to shatter. A bottle was meant to consume.

Liquidating Perry

Kathleen wrote us letters from Germany, then Iraq. Somehow she had made it into the Army, into Ramstein and Desert Storm.

Not that the Army is getting one's life back together, but trying counts for everything, even more so than success.

Perry intercepted her letters. *For your own good*, he later said, *and mine.*

Liquidating Perry

It was an old house. The fixtures wiggled. It was learning our weight as much as we were learning its.

Out of respect of our new home, Perry told Travis and I, *please confine your fighting to the backyard.*

Houses were to inhabit, not to flip. And unlike people, houses let you know when things were going south. The floor wears out. The paint gives way, flecks off. Windows turn brittle.

I didn't like being read to. Perry didn't read fast enough. He didn't do the voices. He was an interesting and weird dude. It was hard to follow him verbally. He inverted everything.

Smoked like a fish. Drank like a chimney.

The same was true of his input on our homework. His edits were homegrown cues: arrows to nowhere, X-outs, squiggly lines. That was the extent of his interest in our schooling. He was not responsible for our erudition or enervation.

That was our responsibility.

So was everything else.

I'm surprised he didn't ask us to help out with rent.

Liquidating Perry

Regrets are plural, as is money. Perry had plenty of both. He made $119,000 in 1989. Money was just numbers on a spreadsheet to him. He was sure he'd live to see cash become obsolete, and the resurgence of prohibition.

One must think of taking over the family business as an allowance, not an income. He joked that he was *dependently* wealthy. He saw himself as a mere middleman of currency, a pass-through for the dollar, a rest stop for cash. The zeros burned holes in his bank account until his account was like Swiss cheese. He wanted to put our barbeque on hydraulics like the souped-up Oldsmobiles cruising up and down Arrowhead Avenue. He wanted to install a full basketball court in the backyard.

There was no reason to think the good money wouldn't last. There were no clouds on the horizon. There was no horizon.

Liquidating Perry

Childhood is scary. There are noises we can't account for, and shadows, and adults around us with very adult problems.

Our morning noises were adult conversations, about drinking and inflation and the Medfly. Of these, the latter was considered the most dangerous. Mornings were not just talk but smells: burnt coffee, Old Spice, menthols. Perry had no need for an A.M. cocktail shaker. Orange juice and vodka only needed stirring with his index finger, plus ice.

We were the kids with the shovels following the horses crapping in the parade. We said *please* and *thank you*, *miss* and *mister*. When we were asked how it came to pass that we were so polite, adults credited Perry and we secretly credited the summers that Perry sent us away to Ft. Deposit, Alabama, with distant family. Politeness made him look good, and when we didn't make him look good, he revoked our favorite things.

This is where Perry came to a crossroads. Discipline. He didn't know how to, and yet, he did. Not physically, but with tame, hands-free reprimands. Spanking was not in his dialectic. He never raised a hand to us – he only raised his glass. He mimed his slaps on our wrists. It was meant to manipulate us emotionally and it worked. We didn't defy him, and there was no curfew to stay beyond. As for snooping for our shoplifted toys or smuggled-in Hustlers, I'm not sure if he knew how. It wasn't his parental prerogative — it meant tabling his focus on himself — and besides, being in the dark was the place to be.

It was, by Perry's admission, a life of low libido. To the rare sight of a woman on a sidewalk he would catcall.

Hello Betty, he'd yell.

It was not chauvinism, but flattery. The dog doesn't want the cat, or the cat the mouse. It only wants to chase.

After Kathleen we were not craving even a morsel of someone maternal. And he never brought girls home.

I almost wish he had.

No mistresses. No time for them.

No beer pong. No beaches.

His fun was Happy Hour, when he treated the service industry like royalty. His fun was buying a Porsche.

The goal is to implode the archetype of the drunk father. With Perry I'm a partial me, a truncated self. I'm the snake hacked into parts but still rattling, writhing.

This is the pressure of doing something beautiful.

It's the pressure to rehabilitate our last name.

Liquidating Perry

In our household it was not Democrat or Republican – it was Wet or Dry. If you factored in inflation, it was not drinking that was improvident, but keeping your money in savings.

We were Dr. Spock babies, Reagan babies. On weekends when Perry planned on staying home he'd write out a note and sign it and send us out to one of the liquor stores in walking distance to get him cigarettes and fifths. We'd stroll over, cash in hand. The clerks all knew Perry. The sight of us carrying Popov and Kools on the street at seven- and five-years-old merited no comment.

Liquidating Perry

Perry claimed to be lucky in life, so he didn't have to be lucky gambling. He often wasn't.

He gambled on credit. He treated his credit as something he had to spend. He treated credit like cash.

You know what's great about credit cards? he said. *They don't bounce.*

He did not gamble to win. It was not gambling to him, but speculating. There were bets so elaborate it was impossible to enjoy Sundays.

If I don't bet them, then they're just football games, he said.

A more strategic gamble would have been investing in art or in his retirement. Because there's no such thing as intelligent gambling. There's no such thing as a judicious exotic bet.

I never heard him use 'need' or 'want' except in the context of his wagers.

He *needed* points. He *wanted* scoring.

This was my childhood. He kept at gambling, kept losing. For decades the big payoff was just one touchdown, one favorable bounce away.

Liquidating Perry

A hypochondriac has many health scares. Perry's health even at 36 was something of a riddle. He had a skin condition he was trying to manage on his own, replacing regular coffee with decaf, Bud with Bud Light.

Decaf is for weaklings, until you suspect that your eczema is attributable to caffeine.

Coffee and vodka. His body could accommodate one dependency. Not two.

For some men the first drink of the day is a treat. For others it's a retreat.

Perry drank as if he had to repress something unbridled inside himself. He drank and the house and the oil company ran themselves into tailspins. He would not attribute any of this to his drinking.

At first, vodka was only something he did in the morning, a way of spritzing up his OJ, a solution to his withdrawals.

It was part of my morning routine also. His hands shook, violently. I held his elbow as he brushed his teeth and put in his contact lenses. I learned to shave him, button up his shirts.

You look handsome, I told him one morning.

His eyes were still bright then. He tucked in his shirt.

Flattery will get you everywhere, he said.

Liquidating Perry

It was a fine time to grow up. There were summer days so gorgeous I wished the house was a convertible, top down. The Dream that Perry was born into was not only alive and attainable, it was ripe for the picking. For him, a knowledge of our country was paramount to any other knowledge – and later, when at 19 I took my own pilgrimage and slept in Greyhound stations and sat next to felons and lovers on the lam, I didn't have the heart to report the despondency back to Perry – as it turned out, he'd learn it all himself first-hand, soon enough.

He took us on month-long RV rides. He spent his money on events and spectacles. There were California Angels games, L.A. Dodgers games. Baseball stadiums weren't supposed to be pretty – the nicer ones to Perry were like warts on the national pastime. As a gambler, he prohibited us from cheering for either team. Regional affinities were irrational to Perry. He had no favorites, and the surge of the crowd after a home run was just that. A surge. Noise.

A year after he died, National Public Radio asked me for a segment about Perry. They wanted something with a "fantastic twist."

The first embellished piece I sent them was apparently too plausible, so I sent them something even more untrue, none of which happened, at least not sequentially.

I said that at our first Angels game, Perry was double-fisting Budweisers in the bleachers yelling for a '*seven-run homer*,' which later became a '*nine-run homer*.'

I said that when security came to escort him out, he took off his belt and used it to climb the right field foul pole.

Poise and aplomb were Perry's antithesis. It's what he was averse to.

I said I was proud of him, that it was time his life stopped dovetailing with Hollywood and time it became Hollywood.

Also, the only other thing I'd seen him climb was a keg.

I said that whoever was running the PA system jacked up the volume to coax him down, which was the same logic that had just compelled Manuel Noriega out of his exile in Panama.

I said Perry's pride was a conundrum. There was so much of it. He couldn't put it away. The only place for it to go was up.

I said that when they finally apprehended him, the guards were quite rough. '*You'll pay for this*,' they told Perry.

But he had not lost his defiance, or his insouciance. "*I'll pay for this?*" he said. "*Put it on my tab.*"

NPR did not like this either. The "loser father" angle did not resonate with them.

Liquidating Perry

Sports, because miracles happen in sports. Not in the office. Not at school.

A man carrying a football fifteen yards across a white line matters to millions of people. I played quarterback growing up because I found the pocket safer than home. It didn't collapse as often.

Sports were not the study of muscles but of Perry's emotions. He didn't fraternize with the coaches or parents. On the sidelines he was free to roam, stalk the action. It was more of his style to storm the field. Bump the umpire in the chest. Kick dirt onto home plate.

Even when we did win, there were no atta-boys from him. No praise. Egos needed deflating, and uniforms were to be dirtied. If we came home with a clean one, what were we doing? Didn't we hustle?

Winning was one thing, and bragging another. Bragging was the parent's prerogative. Our achievements reflected on Perry, not us. Winning meant learning how to lose badly, not sorely. He had no tolerance for tears, or any ability to console. No matter what happened, however terrible – and this was true for any adversity – it was unpatriotic for us to cry.

Liquidating Perry

I worry that I'm underwriting Travis, who was a big part of Perry's final years because Perry couldn't crack the nut of their mutual aversion.

With a new technology something is always breaking, and when the Card-Gard was updated in 1990 Perry had a hard time adjusting. He had inherited Leo's thirst but not his business acumen. He started using 'hope' quite a bit when talking about the repairs. So much of his sales hopes became 'God willing,' or 'fingers crossed.'

I could see he was about to snap. I wasn't sure on whom. I hoped it would be on me.

That year Travis and I waged a united front against parental dictatorship. Perry, for example, did not like my cracking my knuckles. It caused arthritis. I did it anyway, a small coup.

Later, Travis elected to run away from home for a week. He made it four blocks. At that age, he couldn't have known that running away is a round-trip proposition.

It was Perry's second milestone: Parenting in Absentia.

He was articulate about his needs in that he didn't talk about them, he just did them and did not apologize for them.

I never heard him say *I'm sorry* until the day I was married.

I'm not writing this as Perry would like. I'm singing too many of his praises. This is a rumination, not a play-by-play. I'm doing to him what he didn't want, what he hoped would never happen.

Children, whose fault it never is, still feel responsible for a parent's foibles, as if they could have done more, as if they were capable of parenting their parents at five years old.

Perry loved his foibles. He hoisted them on us.

He was opaque in our childhood. You could only see the outline of him, like the mist in bad horror films.

He was not a shape-shifter as much as he was a scene-stealer.

Perry made friends with the haves, but had more fun with the have-nots. He was thorny. Then again, every bar needs a gadfly. He liked sitting there in the dark and the dim, saying smart things, being an aphorist. But after a few drinks he slurred, and his smart things were garbled, like the unintelligible drivel one sputters coming out of a dream.

Lacerating his liver with whiskey, not because it calmed him, but the opposite. It electrified him. It was hard for him to do anything while he was drinking, except do more drinking.

Start drinking, he would mutter into his pillow. *Can't stop.*

Liquidating Perry

A hangover was the closest he could get to death on a daily basis. He didn't know how dearly he would pay for it later. It was wholesale dependency with ineffective splashes of cold turkey. He replaced double whiskeys with double wheatgrass shots. He tried O'Doul's. He experimented with horseradish in his Bloody Marys. He tried smaller sips, grog rations. None of it worked. He didn't blame alcohol – he blamed how good it made him feel. He started referring to his chances of recovery as his bookie would his weekend bets. Recovery was a long shot, +900, with 9-1 odds against. Relapse was a sure thing, -700, 2/5.

Liquidating Perry

    California is not just redwoods and poppies to me, it's a roulette of bars – Ye Olde Lamplighter, The Rustic Inn, The Wooden Nickel, The Greenbriar. It was considered poor form not to drive drunk a generation ago, but to get caught doing so. I cringe only when I think about Perry's good fortune behind the wheel, because of what could have happened, and how, even though none of it was my fault – so say my friends, counselors, experts – I would have been complicit because there was something that chased him out of the house after work, to the point at which he bypassed the house completely, and I swear that between age 7 and 9 I have no memory of my father, not because I have blocked it out or because I choose not to, but because, as Travis so eloquently put it, the bastard wasn't there.

Perry did not wear his heart on his sleeve. He wore it on ours. And we wore it out.

His story is all true and it is also too good to be true. There are some good memories. I like to be alone with them. I can't treasure them if I talk about them.

Never rob a young man of his sentimentality. He parts with it so soon, as it is.

Liquidating Perry

Rochambeau was the great adjudicator in our household.

Paper covers rock. Scissors cut paper. The common denominator is paper.

We counted to three. We made fists. Perry wanted us to be Renaissance kids, to do everything and effortlessly. We were to hit baseballs 300 feet and golf balls 300 yards. But it wasn't to teach us fitness or discipline or patience or ethics. A round of golf took four hours. For Perry, this was cheaper than the going rate for babysitting.

Liquidating Perry

Sour cream came in *dollops*. Salt came in *pinches*. Perry was not a baker.

There was the year he gave me the traveling salesman machine that he used to peddle lubrication products for my science fair project. I learned the ins and outs of viscosity. In comparison, baking soda volcanoes were lowbrow.

He never lost his hyperbole. Exaggeration was the best part of his stories, and there was an AP Style we grew up on unique to the Amendts, a classy way of phrasing things that gave us room to use slang, rampantly if we wanted, just so long as we explained the slang to Perry, gave him context, used it in a sentence for him. The top 40 was the *hit parade*. The living rooms of mobile homes were *parlors*. Bars were not bars but *establishments*. Drunks weren't drunks; they were patrons.

Even Kathleen was not Kathleen. She was *your mother*.

Liquidating Perry

Christmas was not Perry's holiday. Holidays were a hardship. They perturbed him. All of them.

I think the Christmas season was almost not commercialized enough for him. He was hard to shop for, impossible. He objected to icicle lighting. He fell behind with his Advent Calendar. He was not much into nog.

He was the patriarch who did not keep the hearthfires burning, but who kept them extinguished. Where are all of the ornaments we made? (For that matter, where's my baby blanket? Birth certificate? Baptism record?) He was the kind to decorate, not to take down and stow the decorations. It was our job to dismantle the holidays. He wanted to keep them up all year. It was not sloth, but festivity.

Somehow he got his tree the day before Thanksgiving. Trees were $35 then – they may still be in some parts of the country. A Christmas tree lot, he liked to point out, was always a Christmas tree lot, even when it was vacant, all year round. He liked the perfume of the trees, their heft. A man should be taller than his tree, Perry believed. Our star was not a tin-foil star but a Dodgers cap. He would have moved the entire operation into his bedroom, if not for the fireplace in the living room and the social currency of its quaintness, like a deep tan after a weekend in Palm Springs: the skirt of the tree and the senile (and, in Perry's absinthe years, faintly anise smelling) German shepherd by the fire and the haphazardly wrapped presents.

We attempted to make wreaths. We were boys. We failed.

Perry had stolen an inflatable life vest from under the seat of an especially wretched flight. We pulled the tab. It blew up into a gaudy yellow. That was our wreath one year.

63

Liquidating Perry

It pained Perry to stay up late on the 24th to pretend to be Santa Claus. He took bites of, then spat out, the brownies we had charred. He said the reindeer would need carrots, peeled. He said Santa preferred 2%.

Santa couldn't make it through the chimney, Perry argued, so would I swing by the locksmith on my way home from school, and make him an extra set of keys?

Come to think of it, Santa might also need a package of Tums.

One year there was actual coal in our stockings. I can't recall where we went wrong, except for a losing season in soccer.

Also, could we leave out a snifter of whiskey for Santa? Why? Because the reindeer are not always compliant.

He knew it was Christmas when everyone who owed him money wouldn't pay up. Christmas was not like Easter when Perry planned elaborate adult egg hunts with jelly beans in some plastic eggs and a healthy bud of marijuana in others. It was unlike Independence Day when he chartered a houseboat at Big Bear and let it drift past the buoys and against the rules into the middle of the lake, under the fireworks, excited by the falling ash and the idea that we could go up at any time.

The holidays were catered affairs with deviled eggs and BBQ platters from Armadillo Dan's. We didn't do holiday cards. The camera did not steal Perry's soul as much as it revealed too much of it.

There are no pictures of you, he told me. *You'll remember more of life the less you photograph it.*

He was more excited by the Indianapolis 500, the Republican National Convention, the television specials that revealed Elvis' true whereabouts. His holidays were the unification bouts, the Wrestlemanias. He didn't have to decorate for those. It was Pay-Per-View. All he had to do was dial it in.

Liquidating Perry

I remember him pouring drinks in December. Pouring. Pouring.

The tree is thirsty, he said. *Like its owner.*

He named the tree 'Perry.' He left it up past New Year's. Come August, the mistletoe was still tacked above the front door.

Chapter Four – Advertisements of Himself

In 1990 Perry's face was a cartography of burst capillaries. When he came across images of authorities raiding underground distilleries from during Prohibition – all those bottles busted by all those zealous axes – it made him want to cry.

Because if this is about his drinking, it needs to be on every page.

Liquidating Perry

We don't get to choose our parents. We are like gumballs out of a machine.

Perry was Mr. Albeit, Mr. Everything Happens to Me. I liked him. He was hard to like. Our relationship was like financial aid. It was on a need basis.

I was six when I started having a certain embarrassing difficulty in the mornings. He was a single parent but it was not his job to play Mr. Mom.

Perry?

Yes, my son?

I blurted it out. I didn't know the word for it was 'erection.'

I don't know what to do with it, I said.

You sound concerned.

I am.

Why? Perry shrieked. *Enjoy it!*

We ate a lot of Wonder Bread.
It's good for you, Perry said. *It's made in a factory. It's enriched.*
He might as well have just said: *It does a cholesterol good.*

Liquidating Perry

For many alcoholics the drinking is the collapse. For Perry it was a symptom of something else, of many unspeakable things.

I'm not overstating his intake. It was a quart of liquor a day – vodka, aquavit, he didn't discriminate – which is two pints, a fifth of a gallon. Which is too much, however you measure it.

This narrative isn't the pain of Perry or his hurt, or his relapse and his conquering it. It is, instead, a marvel at his foolhardiness. There was the folly of his attempts at organization, the slow death of his resolutions. There was his ambivalence about work. It was exasperating and at the same time endearing. He was not a procrastinator but a filibusterer.

Why do today what you can put off until tomorrow?

On Monday, there is no such thing as Friday. It is so far away. Perry had to gird himself up for Mondays. His attitude was similar to Joseph Heller's hero in *Something Happened*: if you walk around the office holding a single piece of paper, no-one will ever bother you. Same is true if you're the boss' son. At the office he had a heavy stout desk and a comfy leather chair, but he preferred standing. All standing is makeshift, Perry's especially. He believed a human should stay upright, learn on his feet. He used the chair when his feet were tired. In meetings he doodled sketches for a standing car.

Any success – all success, in fact – was attributable to hard work, which was not working really but loitering in the office the longest. It astonished him that unpleasantness was seemingly incentivized in business circles. He guessed that people enjoyed being bullied. It upset him that the prevailing executive focus was not on philanthropy but philandering.

It was not a glass ceiling at Amendt Oil but a popcorn ceiling. He installed tile in the hallways so he could hear his staff approaching, in heels. It was not misogyny but the reverse. He cultivated insubordination among his secretaries. Their jobs were not on the line, no matter how poor their performance. He gave them no choice – through good pay and treatment – to work for anyone but him. He gave them Fridays off. He let them babysit us.

Perhaps he wasn't the man for the job, but it was his job. He said the darnedest things for money. It was a pet peeve of his and a perturbation.

You know what money can't buy, Zachary.

Happiness? I guessed.

No, Perry said. *The New York Yankees.*

Liquidating Perry

Most Baby Boomers are square or round pegs. Perry was another shape altogether.

If I am remarkably candid in here then he survives, but if I pull my punches and hedge my bets and write him with an airbrush like the celebrities on the gossip magazines, then you'll have only gotten a fraction of Perry, when there was more than enough of him to go around.

Our jobs were to answer the phone during James Bond marathons, to grow up not to be astronauts but 007s. We likened everything to cartoons, the old Warner Bros' Mel Blanc-narrations. For instance, Perry's business competition was Elmer Fudd. At night he was not a whirlwind, but the Tasmanian Devil.

He wasn't around to monitor homework. He just presumed that these things were being accomplished. No bad grade would be construed by him as a cry for help, but as a wholesale failure.

Cognitively I was good for one hour of assignments a day. Any more and I became dissonant, faint. It's hard to be satisfied with such a child. Not impertinent. Not disrespectful. But entitled. I wanted my gifts manifested into magnificence, immediately. I'm sure I reminded Perry of his younger self, and that it terrified him.

If prostitution was the first profession then tending bar was the second. His fantasy was a bar where he could take his wife and his mistress, when he had neither, when wedding rings were just costume jewelry to him. He was better off as a bachelor, a suburban dilettante, a bon vivant of the cul-de-sacs. He treated the suburbs like his own snow globe, his purview, his domain.

I wish it was always nighttime, he said more than once.

Or, as he famously put it, *It's 5 a.m. somewhere*. I have stockpiled Perry, morsel by morsel. I try to soften his blows, because I'm the soft landing he couldn't afford in his infirm years, when he crashed.

Liquidating Perry

    I never saw him dance. It doesn't mean he never danced. There was a lot of Perry I didn't see.
    It's hard when people look up to you. It's almost unfair. His friends should have had to ask for permission first. Perry recycled his profits back into his body and theirs, not by way of tanning or tattoos but good liquor for himself and any stragglers who showed up on our doorstep despondent, thirsty, in need of that ineffable something that was stabilizing about Perry's advice.
    What's funny about Perry-as-oracle-or-Perry-as-psychologist is that he didn't listen. He stared out into space. And when confronted, he blamed an excess of earwax.

Liquidating Perry

Age does something to your idea of your extraordinariness, but Perry's was something of an exception. He was a solicitor of destiny, in that he saw his fate and asked for a reprieve and threw a tantrum when it wasn't granted.

He was the quintessence of the terrific, capable drinker. He felt ardently about ardent spirits. Whiskey was like coffee to him – a stimulant, a must-have.

He would rather live with drink than live with the withdrawals.

The drunk side of Perry was a façade. It was not the real him. It was an alibi for the small things, like fracases and vertiginous stumbles and waking up with mysterious bruises. It was also a mask, and masks were meant to scare away the gods, not loved ones.

I think he was approximately alcoholic. I don't think even he could define his dependency. The perception of his success – or the degree to which he could handle his intake – was all predicated (as it is now) on holding down a job, maintaining a social status, money. To Perry's friends, he was alright until he couldn't pick up the checks. Only then was he not alright. Only then did he have a drinking problem.

Drink dulls and elevates. Drink amplifies. Drink babysat Perry while we were at soccer practice, at school. Without fail he would get the hiccups. It was a nightly ritual, a strange liturgy. I would help stand him on his head and, at his insistence, sock him in the stomach.

Harder, he'd say, upside-down, where a grimace looks like a grin.

Liquidating Perry

I was Elvis for Halloween in the third grade. My hair was saturated in Aqua Net and I had an ice-cream scoop for a microphone. I went out trick-or-treating with friends while Travis was hospitalized for choking on a Wheat-Thin.

Childhood is finite because there is so much to omit. So much is fuzzy.

For example: a child is pinned under a garage door. Travis. It's crushing him. A stranger driving by in a Datsun truck sees him, stops, pulls him out and drives off.

That was on a Tuesday, I think.

The architecture of a life. Move some walls around. Add a second bathroom.

Perry wasn't a man; he was a guy. He was the opposite of handy. It was not DIY but RIY – Ruin it Yourself. Home repair was not best left to the experts in his eyes, but to the lowest bidders. He didn't teach us to shave, or later how to drive. We'd figure it out eventually, on our own.

Liquidating Perry

These are the furlongs of life. Years are not units of time; they're vintages.

It takes a little clairvoyance to piece Perry all together. I'm the custodian of his life now. This is meant to reconstitute him, because my childhood memories are not just melting, they are an ice cube dropped into three fingers of premium gin, as syrupy as the wake of a cruise ship, or like the warm mist in classic movies when the heroine faints.

He drank when he felt like it, which was seemingly always. It was that ethereal thing in his gut that goaded him on, some kind of internalized peer pressure, as if his conscience was bullying him.

Moderate drinking wasn't enough. Moderation was no way to do anything. Moderation was bad advice.

He drank to get to a certain place he couldn't find or name and never arrived at. He enjoyed drinking. It calmed him. Plus, he rationed it. It was like a nightcap, taken like medicine, every half-hour. It was clockwork.

Except he wasn't good at it. It didn't make him bombastic, or affectionate. He was a cauldron and the drinking tipped the pot.

I don't know why he did it. I never asked. As if there's only one reason, or only twenty reasons. Whatever reasons he had were his. They were none of our business.

Liquidating Perry

It's not what happened that matters, but the sequence in which it did.

In 1991 we were in a car accident on the way to school. It was 8 a.m. I was brushing my teeth in the front seat.

Either Perry ran the red or the other guy did.

Perry's breath was hot and astringent and it confused the cops when he passed the field sobriety test.

Liquidating Perry

You can talk your way out of a traffic citation, but you can't argue your way through a metal detector.

That year we visited Tombstone, Arizona. Flying out of Sky Harbor they detained Perry because I had snuck a toy pistol in my suitcase.

It runs in the family. It skips generations.

It was also evidence that there are no exceptions. Only rules.

Liquidating Perry

I work all day/get half-drunk at night says the poet Phillip Larkin. Except Perry got all-drunk.

He had no business parenting, but thank God he did.

He was a cold pizza kind of guy. He came home late and ate leftovers. On a digestive level our meals were elegant. His evenings were not for eating but for being 'on.' The vacation was never over. Every day was a binge. He was one of those drivers who didn't belong on the road after a certain hour, and when his Chrysler was stolen and used in a bank robbery and totaled in the getaway, it was a bit of relief to know Perry was on foot.

He did not patronize bars; he haunted them. After a six-pack he became ghoulish. It was the art of eavesdropping on two conversations at once. He gorged on rancid mescals and vomited in stained ceramic urinals. He got confused when he came home because he blacked out and didn't remember what he promised or to whom. At times his friends goaded him to get up and sing The Star Spangled Banner during karaoke.

I can't sing, he said, *but I do, but I shouldn't*.

Bars were for killing time, annihilating the days. Perry thought it was his sole source of fun, his only antidote to boredom. He should have stayed home. Without him the house was in disarray. Feral cats pissed on the washing machine in the garage and there were spiders all over the lawn furniture.

He not once apologized for being gone. For Catholics, guilt is outgoing as well as incoming. And Perry's job was not to alleviate his guilt, but to help us with ours.

Liquidating Perry

There is no language for vodka. Vodka isn't supposed to taste like anything.

The nights of 1992 he not only drank, he committed political sabotage. Clinton was polling higher than Bush, and there were only so many Democratic bumper stickers Perry could turn upside down in the neighborhood before he got caught.

It wasn't just Democrats. Dandruff, also, was the enemy. He started wearing white shirts instead of dark ones. He wore more seersucker and got rid of the body-length mirrors in the house. He was not in love with his image – at least, not below the neck. This was vanity of the first order, the first rank.

Dandruff, I think, was the harbinger.

Perry's dead and to this day he still upends my plans. He has the power to throw my present-day asunder. It's as if he knew my greatest fear was a scenario wherein a child (my unborn son or daughter) takes interest in his grandfather (Perry), dismayed that there is not only no biography available, but no record of him existing at all.

In this vein, I don't wish Perry had kept a journal. It'd have been a contrivance. But we were meant to live prominently, with lucid and long paper trails.

So I labor and slog, stretching like taffy the limbs of my family tree.

We were growing up. Leo and Eloise were getting old.

Getting old was shopping for hearing aids, prosthesis. You did not pray for wealth anymore, but to remain continent.

Leo's heart failed in 1993. We spread his ashes in a creek that was later identified as factory runoff.

(Eighteen years later, the day before he died, Perry gave a stool sample at a hospital in Indio, CA. *This isn't my best work*, he told the nurses.)

Eloise's breast cancer overtook her less than a year later. She had outlived Leo, which I think was her goal all along.

Even more telling about her character: she had lied about her age on her life insurance policy.

The oil business, for various reasons, was the next to go.

The reasons were Big Oil, the Seven Sisters who lobbied for environmental upgrades they could afford, but which mom-and-pop operations couldn't.

That eggs are counted in baskets in the first place is a crime. Perry tried to keep the company solvent. He had a great respect for quotas. Quotas made him wealthy, prolific.

Until all of his suddenly evaporated.

Liquidating Perry

He had no idea how slowly everything could unravel. If it had happened all at once I think he'd have recovered. It was as if he couldn't believe such a slow cascade of bad luck.

He could push himself up 100 times a day, but he couldn't pull himself up.

Perry's life fell apart where he was most vulnerable: at the seams. His teeth became harder to help him brush. After twenty minutes he quit trying to put in his contacts.

Ignore, he quivered. *Move on.*

Latchkey parents are much maligned, but I think if they got together at some sort of annual convention they'd praise themselves for inadvertently raising self-reliant children. It begs the question as to what degree Travis and I were complicit in allowing Perry to stunt his maturity because we were able to cook for ourselves, microwave for ourselves, babysit ourselves.

But then he'd come around again and miss us, or we him, and suddenly we'd have a steady diet of our father.

Without work Perry got to be by himself, which was the hardest company for him to keep. Drinking was now not just for Friday nights or weekends, but for Tuesday afternoons and Wednesday mornings.

Sobriety was the other side of the fence, with barbed wire. The grass was not greener. The other grass looked boring.

He bought a used Chevy. His biggest fear became drunk driving. Not because he was concerned for others, but because he could no longer afford the fines.

He would not admit that the family company folded. He said he needed a year off. He took not one year, but four. He started out enthusiastically with pet projects, such as collecting vinyl. He was the guy driving around picking up the records people were leaving out on the streets upon the advent of the compact disc.

All he could do is what he did. If your father had a vice or compulsion, I hope it was a toolshed, or a hot-rod, or birdwatching, anything but Perry's.

This could be the night, he said, every afternoon.

It was his slogan. Later, in New York, it became my slogan.

It wasn't just a catch-phrase, of course. It was the title of a 1955 film with Paul Douglas and Jean Simmons. Who wasn't just an actress, but a famous drinker in her own right, and, by a twist of fate, Kathleen's roommate for two months during her stay at the Betty Ford Clinic.

Liquidating Perry

I didn't think anything could be smaller than rehab. But the world, apparently, is.

I wonder what the ladies discussed. Perry, addiction, mascara. I doubt Travis or I ever came up.

Liquidating Perry

To have a front row seat to a parent's decline doesn't mean you can participate or influence the action. You are relegated to watch.

People and alcohol are adept at obscuring problems. I represent the fourth generation of a family of heavy drinkers – a statement that reads to me now as if I am part of a large Olympic delegation – and where the national average for longevity is increasing steadily, the Amendts' is plummeting on a filial level.

Especially the males.

Aware of this trend, in 1995 Perry experimented with quitting. (He did all the things they advised you not to try at home.) But cocktails were, it turns out, calories he couldn't do without. There was sweating and sleeplessness the first day, the fetid humidity of my evaporated night-terrors, irritability and grogginess the second, an impenetrable mental fog the third. By day four it's as if he had never taken a drop, until he saw everyone else drinking and the fun he was missing out on. On day five his liver starts to hurt from lack of attention. Day six never comes.

When the body says *enough* but the thirst must be slaked, you hope for a steady hand and a stronger spouse, neither of which Perry had. He was 40, he was 41, too young for such bodily and spiritual harm, hemorrhaging money, in and out of alcohol. He spent all he had saved and inherited. Retirement became an unattainable, ephemeral thing. Buried treasure became his retirement plan. As did the Lotto.

If wishes were horses, he said, *I'd ride*.

My instant coffee years, he later called them. *My Velveeta years*.

It was classic Perry. He could grin, but deep down, he could not bear it.

Chapter Five – Uphill Two Bottles with Four Miles of Wine

I love this story about Perry.

During intermission of one of the annual premieres of The Nutcracker at Berdoo's California Theatre – my aunt was the artistic director for many years – Perry queued up with a line of johns waiting for a urinal.

Someone jumped the line in front of him.

Perry kept his cool and tapped the guy on the shoulder.

It will do no good to confront you about this, he said, *because I know you've been cutting in line your entire life.*

Liquidating Perry

History is neat but it isn't tidy. People die of lies and of tensions.

Perry's was a collapse in two parts, bridged by the most gorgeous sobriety you can imagine.

I know because I was there to see it.

But I was not the reason for it.

It was time for his third milestone: How to Court Women and Be Taken to Court.

On June 6, 1996, after Oscar de la Hoya was decisioned by Julio Cesar Chavez in a close fight in Mexico City, Perry smacked a woman around.

My stepmother.

She will remain nameless.

Perry referred to it thereafter as *D-Day*. For the cops who arrived, it was a slam dunk: frail woman with bruised wrists, and Perry's noxious, potash breath.

Whatever happened, he was in the wrong. He was half-a-husband that night.

My stepmother did not press charges, but she did sue him for divorce, then alimony, out for the money she thought he had saved but that actually didn't exist. Perry mounted an incompetent defense. She held all the chips, in large part because she convinced Perry into taking Kathleen's name off of our birth certificates.

Humans don't break. We shatter. Looking at Perry as he was being deposed, I saw him fractured and apologetic, almost embarrassed about his poor taste and judgment in women.

My stepmother was the kind of person who doesn't clean the lint out of the dryer filter.

I've tried to get Kathleen's name back on my birth records. It's nearly impossible.

Liquidating Perry

I harbor no enmity for the gender: if anything I harbor the reverse. When my wife and I recently made out our wills on a cocktail napkin one inebriated paranoiac evening, we learned that the poor and middle class must manufacture their last wills and testaments out of inferior materials.

I, Zachary Amendt, hereby make Paige Williams, my spouse, the beneficiary of all monies from today into perpetuity. As in, she gets everything. As in, 100%. As in, no one else does.

Words are formulaic, the same as numbers. You can solve the conundrum of your parents just by moving some letters around. Still, Perry did not ask for this and you did not ask for it and as for me, I asked for this so I could expunge Perry, exorcise him. And while I share his story with strong fear and dread, it's not as though I've holed myself in a basement the past two years drinking Robutussin.

Money is like memory and it's like cupping water. It doesn't matter how tight you hold it. Somehow it slips through.

Perry's falling out of favor was his doing and it was his undoing. He made it hard to root for him. He lost his will power, his gumption. It was real actual grief, cannot-get-out-of-bed-grief, can't-eat-grief. Throwing the covers off in the morning and love of any kind was a Sisphyean endeavor – even his love for us.

Liquidating Perry

One night he tried making a list of things he was grateful for. After fifteen minutes of nothing, he gave up.

Liquidating Perry

What's an alcoholic's favorite drink? he quizzed me that night.

You're not an alcoholic, I told him.

Water, he said.

Perry didn't mind being nickeled, or even dimed. However, divorce was like being Benjamined.

Very smart people are often quite stupid with money. It was not that he had a hard time articulating his financial needs, but that he had so many they couldn't be itemized, or even ranked. He became something of a professional houseguest for a year. Being a great guest meant staying out of sight. It meant stripping the sheets off the bed when you left. People are not only aborted in the womb, but sometimes after they're born, after you befriend them, once they love you. His impoverishment was a test of his friends' generosity, of how much of a burden he could be.

It was the commencement of his fourth milestone: Unmaking Friends.

They quickly tired of Perry's freeloading and negativity.

He who had let them freeload. He who had spent all of his optimism on them, for years.

He thought they hated him but it was worse than that: they stopped thinking about him.

Drinking buddies and true friends, he told me over the phone. *One day you'll have to learn the difference.*

Liquidating Perry

Nothing matches that first drink. Until the second one. Then the third. Until the twelfth.

The cocktail shaker imparted a faint metallic taste onto his martinis, not unpleasant, a bit like what Perry imagined hemlock or arsenic to taste like. For his entire life it had been coffee for the effect and liquor for the taste. After the divorce and his parents dying the two were reversed. Even his language for drinking changed. *He did a good job on it* or he *polished it off* – 'it' being a bottle a night, when it used to be half-a-bottle.

He started hanging out at the American Legion, which I remember chiefly for its flat sugary tonics and the commander who had memorized everyone's war record, so no one could exaggerate their exploits. Perry walked in every morning at 11 a.m., mockingly, as if trumpets announced his arrival. He was a lively participant on Bingo Night.

The veterans were heroes with hard faces and meager pensions.

Slowly they ostracized Perry.

He had asked for too many pints on credit, too many comped drinks.

He was gossiped about, pitied.

They thought he had money stashed away in the Cayman Islands.

That part was hilarious to Perry. Money. He couldn't even find it on a map.

My stepmother, also, thought he had money offshore.

It didn't take long for the back alimony to exceed six figures. The total became something of a joke to Perry. There were no wages to garnish, or accounts to raid. How much higher could the number get?

He hoped it would eclipse $1 million.

Liquidating Perry

Homelessness just sort of happened, he said.

I don't want to loiter too long in this part of his past. It was not a roofless elysium. There were, I can only imagine, hundreds of small scams or diversions he orchestrated to stay alive. He suddenly relied less on his touch and taste than on what he called his seventh and eight senses: intuition and déjà vu. He developed an animosity to privilege, as if he hadn't paid cash for his house in a bull economy, as if Leo didn't pay for his first roadster at Aquinas. Being itinerant was not a quality of life but a lifestyle. Staples and basics like coffee became delicacies. He maintained a great deal of personal and professional obscurity, especially to his creditors. It was his uncomplainingness, which was not stoicism but martyrdom. He assured us, from pay phones or strangers' mobile phones, or phones at bars, that all was okay when it wasn't, when it very much was not okay.

Most descents are slow, gradual. Not his. It was rapid. He plummeted. Still, there can be an aesthetic to a tailspin, as there was with Perry. Life was finally what it wasn't in movies. He was a student of films; he knew how not to let the Hollywood bauble hypnotize him.

Come 1996 Perry was living in a treehouse on the playground where Travis and I went to pre-school. He named it Fort Apache, after the film, also starring John Wayne. After dark he would jump the fence and lay out his gear. It was real wood, fully enclosed, and cozy.

It's the best secret in town, he said. It was not homelessness to him, but camping.

The fates of lives are dissected by fractions, degrees. One morning Perry had the misfortune of sleeping in. The children rushed in and found him scrambling for his clothes. That afternoon the administrators – my former teachers – installed barbed wire around the playground. He returned to Wildwood Park, under the eucalyptus and on the bleachers where, thirty years earlier, Leo and Eloise cheered him on during Pony League games.

Liquidating Perry

It is not incredible that he lived so long in such squalor. Suicide never occurred to him. I think he knew that if he tried he would foul it up somehow. Plus, he couldn't afford to kill himself. To do it well took money that he didn't have.

A propensity for drink is like a deformity you don't realize you have until adulthood.

Still, what is true of Perry is not true for me, not all of it. I get into the same trouble, only worse – into notoriety, not piety.

High school for me was mostly unmentionable, except for my fake ID. I was jealous of my friends because they were like Morrissey, protracted with angst, while I had none, no edge whatsoever. I wore khaki pants. I lettered in debate.

Perry's homelessness was a timelapse of my emotional growth. He had been a mainstay until he disappeared. If anyone asked I said he was 'retired,' which wasn't untrue, or I said 'homeless,' which was. They all thought I was joking about his situation. They too assumed the Cayman Islands.

Perry defied life, staying off the grid, inaccessible. His solution to not keeping up his relationships in those years was to have none. Except with me.

Incrementally is the only way Perry revealed himself. He fed me scraps of himself, crumbs.

Charity isn't mandatory, you learn, especially when it you that needs it. Perry was stoic about his situation, but I knew it was an artifice. Selfishly he did not ask for more help, though it would have done him infinite good.

Help is hard, he said. *Asking feels so premeditated.*

Perry became a burden on taxpayers, but a small burden. He didn't use all of his food stamps. His clothes no longer fit him. I gave him my used shirts. Not hand-me-downs, but hand-him-ups.

His liver was gassed. His heart was a contrivance. He was incapable of seeing his future and would dispute whether or not he had a future at all. Alcohol became even more of an escape, the rare times he could find it. Not that he had to be 'on' anymore after a few drinks – only that, when I asked him why he continued, he had nothing to say except:

You know, you're not better than me.
I don't act like I'm better than you, I told him.
Well, you're not, he huffed.

Perry's forties remind me of something John Berryman wrote about aging:

I sat by fires when I was young
now I'm old I do the same
only now
I do it more slowly.

Nothing I find can tarnish my opinion of him. Then again, he isn't exactly on a pedestal. He told many lies. Yarns, after all, were meant to be spun. It was like when San Bernardino's former mayor, Al Ballard, lived with us, bragging about his and Leo's old graft.

Take whatever dollar figure he gives you, Perry said, *and divide by 5 if you want the truth.*

The day I turned 21, Perry bought me a beer. It was unusual. I didn't know where he got the cash. I was the one always buying.

You have an older brother, he said.

It was a girl he met near Loch Ness on his first trip abroad in 1975. Affairs can't not be torrid, and characteristically he took no precautions. When he and Kathleen went on their first trip overseas six years later, they took a flight to Berlin on Lufthansa back when the rows faced one another. Across from them was a cute young family – a proud father who looked nothing like his son, and that girl from Scotland.

I did the math, Perry said. *The poor guy. Your mother had just told me she was with you. I felt quite virile on that flight.*

Why'd you tell me this now? I asked.

He took a pull from his Budweiser and ordered two shots of tequila, Cuervo, the Gold.

The more you know, he said.

Liquidating Perry

Shawnee, Kansas, was Perry's middle-age rebellion. It was also the only state at the time where he could get his driver license. California had revoked it on account of his alimony. How he was to drive to a job that would pay for the alimony without a license ... we left that logic up to the politicians in Sacramento.

Kansas was something of an uptick in his life. He took a job at Wal-Mart. It was a new world for him, not making decisions but taking orders, polishing floors, folding onesies, picking up swing shifts. There was no shame in his putting away his pride, but he still declined employee recognitions and merit raises.

Keep it, he told his supervisors. *Mr. Walton needs it.*

In Shawnee he started attending, for the first time, Alcoholics Anonymous.

It was his fifth milestone, and my favorite one: The Treasure That is Not in The Bottle.

Liquidating Perry

Please don't say *'rehab,'* he told me. *You know I hate abbreviations.*

Apple cider vinegar instead of applejack. Vanilla ice cream instead of vanilla extract.

Day-by-day is the worst and the only way to fix these troubles. (The temptation is part of the drama. Will he or won't he relapse?) He was a reluctant audience at first. He sat in the back. They relied on him to arrive early and get the coffee started.

It was the same in Palm Springs, where he ended up in 2006 after one of Leo's friends offered him a one-way train ticket home.

You can't take the California out of the man or back alimony out of your bankruptcy proceedings. It was like taking a tomahawk to his golden years. His time in the Coachella Valley – as clearheaded as he was, as optimistic, as forward-thinking – were broke years, so unlike what he had envisioned for himself, living high off the hog, driving a Mercedes, a suite at the Palm Canyon Inn, golf in Indian Wells, drinks with the surviving Rat Pack. The dollar was less elastic there. His needs were so prodigious they were almost not worth mentioning.

You should get an extra point on your credit score for every credit card you don't sign up for.

The thing about cold turkey is that it isn't expensive. Cold turkey is free and free was Perry's favorite price.

His transfer between Wal-Marts didn't pan out. He hoofed it for part-time work. His idea of job-searching was making the rounds with a folder full of crisp resumes. I can picture him because one day I went along with him. Not slovenly, always put together, but hanging by a thread … like a marionette it wasn't about the thinness of the thread Perry was hanging by, but its strength. His suit was threadbare and from the Salvation Army. He doused the musty smell of his jacket with musk. His crisply starched shirt wilted in 30 minutes in the desert heat. His knees like the hinges of his eyeglasses creaked, from abuse, not disuse.

It was an argument against perambulation. Even with his credentials it seemed he could only move backwards. He found the customary dead-ends. He did not call attention to his graduate study or two decades of managerial experience; they were not transferable skills, apparently.

He got himself a pay-as-you-go mobile phone, for the phone screenings.

No, I can't account for that gap in my resume.

He had a lot of explaining to do. It was not the world he had grown accustomed to.

I want kudos, he said, when I asked him for his professional objective, for his resume. *Not verbal kudos*, he clarified. *But the granola bar.*

The world is not structured on intelligence quotients. Quite the opposite, it seems.

You can't use me? he asked a recruiter. *I'm not a Phillips screwdriver. Use?*

A job search is like any other unmentionable thing. Graveyards of resumes.

Just following up with a quick hello to confirm your receipt of my personality test results, he said on the school district's general voicemail. *I'm looking forward to discussing the janitorial position further. Did I mention I graduated from Dartmouth?*

It wasn't the speed of modern life that distressed him, but the expendability of so much of the workforce. Eventually he found a job as a substitute teacher. He didn't hate children the first two years. Being a substitute was playing the bad cop, all day, for months. His schedule and errands were scattered all about the valley, which was hard enough to get around in a car, let alone by public bus.

He was boring but sober and that was the important part. I finally had a glimpse of Perry after work, slumped in his recliner, eating ice cream, watching the evening news.

That Perry. The speechless, mute one.

He tried dating, mostly to find a rich widow, but he couldn't muster up the confidence. Clothes, with what money? A haircut with what money? He couldn't so much as afford paper, and was obliged to write down his appointments and grocery lists inside of his passport.

It's not like I'm ever going to use it ever again.

Poverty kept him still. He stayed put in Palm Springs. It was a question of his wherewithal against his wanderlust. For him to move forward as someone okay with himself he had to discard any thought or possibility of a yesterday.

He wasn't a spring chicken anymore, but a summer chicken. His heart started to hop, like a hummingbird's. He checked his pulse so often that I suggested he walk around with a stethoscope.

His health mattered to him. He had learned what it was worth, finally.

Liquidating Perry

It was around this time that he started re-attending Mass. What the Church needed in his opinion was not an organist but a saxophonist. He had stopped going to Mass for decades because, as he put it, *I wasn't sorry for anything I'd done.*

All of this – being on the straight and narrow once again, tempering himself, tuning down his interior volume – was still a revelation to him, and not all that palatable of one. Work was trudgery but there was no better way to spend the hours. He liked having work, but eight hours was too much. He leaned back in his chair, followed the lesson plan. At recess and nap time, he slept. Electronic bells pealed, signaling the final hour, the last ten minutes.

It was a life of jettisoning addictions. Sometimes he allowed himself a nominal amount of fun at night, just to relax, like a square of dark chocolate, no less than 70% cacao. His guilty pleasures had always been inexpellable offenses: the smell of felt pens, gasoline being dispensed, the feel of brand-new socks, the discard pile of gin rummy.

A ritual was important. A ritual was a small win. He tried to laugh at the bad television and be happy with the crossword and just enjoy sobriety. These were tall orders for Perry – too tall, it turned out. The most onerous part of substituting was checking the computer every night to find open teaching assignments. He was new to it, learning it. He was not a quick study.

What's a login? What are cookies?

His password was 0010. It was also the PIN to his bank account. It wasn't strong enough, but he didn't mind. They could mine him for all of his data. He had no credit left to ruin.

Liquidating Perry

  The author should not be present, not even in the wings. But this is where I make a cameo in Perry's life.
  I was 25. You think Perry's example would have motivated me to avoid his lifestyle. The opposite happened: I moved to New York.
  I went there standing up, when I should have approached it on my knees. I flew into Kennedy instead of Newark when LaGuardia was closest.
  Travel is a great teacher. An airport is an airport is an airport.
  Perry once asked for a shovel either to dig to Brooklyn or a vice to clamp the coasts together. There was too much distance between us. The entire country stood in our way. I moved to New York for a girl who brought her opera glasses to the racetrack and tipped the bugler $20 to play a few bars of *When I Fall in Love*. They were the most eventful years of anyone's life. Years of exquisite, elaborate meals. The boroughs, to me, were slums of $5 million homes. We were Scott and Zelda Fitzgerald, 2.0. Adults with childlike fears. Scared of the dark. Of betrayal. Of God. I did with my credit cards what I wasn't supposed to. I paid them off with student loans. I bought myself tattoos. I was not collecting my thoughts, but paychecks. I thought: they will bury me in the history books not with an asterisk next to my name, but a Michelin star.
  All of this while Perry substituted, schlepping his crayons and dry-erase boards from Thermal to Cathedral City. On the phone he seemed more focused on me than on himself. Whatever I was doing 3,000 miles away I should do harder, he advised, unless it was drinking and gambling, because hadn't I learned from him? That we were not inclined to succeed at these things?
  Sometimes this is like taking a diviner to my past, to find where the shame is deepest. To find where to dig. I'm wringing every drop of shame and embarrassment out of myself.

My shame and embarrassment are bottomless.

I think Perry felt his mortality, or else his stamina for sobriety waning. He wanted grandchildren. One day he almost begged for them.

Tell me she's pregnant.

She's not.

Lie to me.

I did lie to him, eventually. On April Fools Day. One expects a prank in the morning, but not in the late afternoon. I told Perry we were expecting. It was the first time I had ever heard him cry.

He was getting better with the computer. He thought of looking up Debbie Huntsman, his first love. Then he thought twice.
What if she's happy?
And say what to her? Marry me? Third time's a charm?
That's the thing about Catholic sacraments. You can't do all of them. Six, at most.

Is it winning *in* marriage, or winning *at* marriage? My wife is a not infrequent reminder that I'm not just Perry's, but Kathleen's as well. I was an expert on my first day of marriage, and today, after 1,310 days of marriage, I am not only a novice, I am the superlative of novice.

Novice-est.

It is a fascinating vantage point, this humbled groom.

I am the person she said she'd never marry: cigars and tattoos, rebellious. But there are no ultimatums anymore, no taboos. It amuses her that I have started wearing ascots, even with flannel shirts. I think it is her patience, her tolerance, which is in no way martyrdom. I'm insufferable at times, but she suffers me. She listens to jazz because she likes jazz clubs and jazz is the essential part of the equation, even though I know it all sounds like the same five songs to her.

She's a Montanan and I'm a Californian, and if you can believe it (I can't) we've never been miniature golfing together.

Marriage is buying her engagement ring at Tiffany's on Fifth Avenue, sweating karats. One learns how expensive it is not to buy the diamond but also to set it. Marriage is not asking for her hand at Rockefeller Center because you've never been ice-skating before, and a proposal of marriage should not involve the risk of bodily harm.

We marry, and they ask us when we're having children. After three years, they stop asking.

She did not want a pony growing up, and yet she plays the ponies. (Whereas the only horses Perry could name were Trigger, Secretariat and the Budweiser Clydesdales.)

Marriage is still a sacrament to me, only it's more secular now, more textured. I'm on lockdown. I'm smitten. I swoon. I swore not to be that guy, and now I am that guy.

Liquidating Perry

I don't mind it; in fact I have manned up to the degree that I feel like I no longer belong to my past, that I was never a bachelor, that I was never not with her.

Marriage. You can malign it. You can quit on it. But right now him – and I hope this is true on my 10,458th day at it him – marriage is the kind of thing I want to blow onto my knuckles and brush against my lapel.

Liquidating Perry

We got married because our names looked good together on the invitations. Perry worried that we wouldn't invite him.

Our inclination was not to. Because there's always something that goes wrong at a wedding, and usually what goes wrong is family.

And for us, it wasn't the napkins or flower arrangements. It was Perry.

In Western tradition the groom is not obliged to pay for his rehearsal dinner the night before his wedding. This is the joy of the groom's father. Perry's joy.

By 2010 Perry was in poor health. He was poor. Our rehearsal dinner was held at Fidel's in Rancho Santa Fe, CA, home of Bing Crosby, where the surf meets the turf. It was gourmet Mexican food, citing our old San Bernardino family dinners at La Mitla or La Paloma, where Travis would order a quesadilla and I tamales and Perry screwdrivers.

Half of the people invited to the dinner hadn't met Perry. He sat on my right.

You have it, right? he asked over the appetizer.

I did have it, $1,000 in cash. Thoughtfulness is a bloodsport to me: there is no one more thoughtful than I: I'm like Dillinger except I kill with kindness.

I held onto it. Still, Perry sweat.

You still have it? he asked over the entree.

I had it. I had it together. I held him up during his toast. *It's my dinner, on me*, he told everyone. *Everyone drink up*, he said. *Top shelf.*

Milestone Six: The Unsustainability of His Sobriety.

Not that sobriety isn't great, but it doesn't boil the blood.

After the rehearsal dinner I found Perry in my hotel room watching re-runs of 'Highway to Heaven' and drinking straight from a bottle of hard-to-find whiskey given to me by my best men.

He said he did it so I didn't have to. He was saving me from myself. I should thank him.

Liquidating Perry

The next day Perry fell during our ceremony. The flower girl was already headed down the aisle. He was bleeding hard from his forehead and we halted the procession and a doctor, my wife's brother, triaged him.

When he finally got to his feet I hugged him like the referees hug fallen boxers, as if to say *It's ok. No more canvas.*

Otherwise it went off without a hitch.

And then he gave us our wedding present: He left before the reception. He disappeared.

It was the best one we received that day. Even better than the four blenders, or the Faberge.

His blood is still on her dress.

Liquidating Perry

I don't know how Perry's memory worked, or if he used it. He seemed unremorseful. He was too proud of having regrets. He freely volunteered them to strangers. It was the first thing you knew about him: What he wasn't. What he had failed at. I think he was more candid about his failures than his successes because he could count his failures and regrets; they were more readily available to him – and besides, few would let him ever forget.

I know, because I was among them.

He also had a lot to hide, and hyperbolizing his failures enabled him to communicate his past through metaphor and innuendo.

Your mother and I were happy and consciously undid our happiness. We untied it like bunting on a present. We discarded the ribbon, he said.

I can't tell you how little this says about him. I'm not evangelizing Perry but liquidating him. I'm not putting his words to paper as much as I'm smothering his words with paper.

Right now I see him as less of the tragic figure as he saw himself.

As my brother, Travis, now sees himself.

The Three Caballeros, Perry called us.

Travis, when he's not teaching his students how to stripe golf balls into the dead-centers of fairways and greens, is teaching them the value of scrambling – hitting from bad lies, from divots and deep grass – because in life as in golf you can't always chip out to safety, you have to bootstrap it and chance it and trust your talent and ingenuity.

These are the sons Perry raised.

I have not always been the best sibling, and vice versa.

He ain't heavy, he's my brother, ain't true.

Chapter Six – The Saint's Blood Liquefies

Old age is regrettable. Old age smells.

We age. Minutiae matter. Interest rate fluctuations matter. Metamucil matters.

Illness is the vengeance. Coffee and cigarettes all day and Canadian Club all night for twenty years, but still it surprised Perry that there were consequences, that he was susceptible to diseases that moved on a parabola ending in his extinction.

Perry neglected himself, not his wants but his actual body. He refused to switch to herbal tea and yoga and die that way, with dexterity and antioxidants, rather than the traditional ways, the whiskey and worry and not exercising. In the final analysis it was a life of infirmity, inexplicable rashes, fatigue. There was such a thing as serious tooth decay.

There was cancer.

Liquidating Perry

Milestone Seven: The Molecular Overdrive That is Lymphoma.

Lymph nodes, it turns out, are not just in your neck. They're everywhere.

I have images of Perry's cancer on a compact disc labeled 'Amendt, P.S., 2012' which I have no plans on opening.

Because his cancer doesn't exist anymore.

He didn't know it was beating him. He thought he had it licked. He wasn't going to name his cancer after something he hated to beat it like that teenager from Michigan who named his leukemia 'Ohio State.' Perry owned his cancer in that he succumbed to it. It undisguised his infirmities, laying them bare like a magician's tricks.

His house at the time was the Coachella Valley Rescue Mission, a homeless shelter run by a faith-based social enterprise. His roommates were mostly ex-cons. He'd call me from the office phone with updates.

Where's the princess!?

The princess had moved back to San Francisco, following the money, just like Woodward and Bernstein.

Perry revealed very little about his treatment. His radiation and chemotherapy were supposed to happen concurrently but he couldn't get a dentist's approval, of all things. It was poor oral health. His gums were sore. Unable to chew, he became reliant on fortified beverages, which was not food (as it is marketed), but drink.

I know cancer did not kill Perry. Ensure killed Perry. Pedialyte killed Perry.

Liquidating Perry

Hardship is relative, as is success, as is abject poverty. (What poverty is not abject?) Perry did not panhandle. He learned to be stealthy on the streets. He learned, in essence, to make himself invisible.

Life is all tea, he said, *and no crumpet.*

Cancer made him do things he'd never done before. He went on an enrollment spree. He wrote letters.

Dear Zachary,
Yesterday's chemotherapy session went well. I feel good. I was approved for Medi-Cal which is good, but, it may delay my radiation because of the change in provider. Oh Well! What else is new? In the meantime I will keep going to chemotherapy. Take care of yourself.
Sorry I did not call you back last night, but I was working in the kitchen when you called. I am doing ok but a little fatigued. I got pissed off at the health care people dragging their feet on my radiation so I issued a formal complaint. It won't do any good, but I'm glad I did it. I will keep you posted. Love You.
Send me an email now and then so I know I have some friends.

Liquidating Perry

I'd like to read this complaint he lodged. Eisenhower Medical Center doesn't want to go down this road, but I do.

The cancer was changing the tenor of his life. He had a sudden surfeit of hope when he started treatment. He thought the cancer was going away.

He was wrong. It was everywhere.

Liquidating Perry

According to Norman Mailer, you always finish a book in worse physical shape than you started it.

It's as if I've let Perry inhabit me for another year, just to purge me of him.

Writing this is like fighting a formidable opponent. Sometimes you have to hit below the belt to finish him.

Zack,

I don't have a phone number for you. Dave from the Mission left a message on our phone and said that Perry was taken to the hospital last night (JFK Hospital in Indio). He said that our name was down as "next of kin" and that the hospital said that he should notify us. I'm really worried and I wanted to be sure you knew. Perry's nurse said that he was "not good". He was admitted very weak and anemic. They have him on an IV and blood to improve his platelets. We were so shocked because he just called last Sunday and he said he was really up and in a good mood. He said that his taste was coming back too.

Your aunt Aleta

Then, as now, Perry's three siblings lived less than one hour away from Palm Springs. But they would not go and see him. One he was estranged from. One had a baby shower to attend. The other's daughters' had a marching band function.

Liquidating Perry

The Sunday before the Tuesday he died – Election Day 2012 – I hustled down to the desert, cancelling my appointments with my San Francisco colleagues who wouldn't understand and didn't care because Perry's health wasn't relevant to their bottom line – you get these people in your life, *employers*, who generously give you three days of paid leave to mourn.

Three days. Pack in your bereavement.

There are people who not only can't face death, but can't entertain it. Perry only looked ready for it because he didn't know it was coming.

He looked relieved when I arrived at Kennedy Hospital (Perry hated acronyms, but when asked, listed his favorite president as *LBJ*.) He didn't know what was going on. All the nurses had told him he was okay. For three days everyone was saying he was alright.

It occurred to me I would have profited from a few episodes of *Grey's Anatomy*. I was handed several DNR authorizations. D̲o N̲ot R̲esuscitate.

Life support isn't one thing or one plug; it's a dozen procedures and interventions. And all I had were intuitions, conjectures.

The nurses X'd places for me to initial.

I wanted to talk to Perry first.

His legs were swollen. He fussed with his catheter. Fear registered in his eyes, which were no longer blue but jaundiced lime. I said hello and he asked me to please kill him and could he have more cold water. I told him I couldn't and daubed his lips with a sponge, until he was hydrated enough to cry.

I didn't think I had the heart. It turns out I did have it, if 'heart' was signing away his life.

Once he fell asleep, I completed the forms. A nurse handed me the carbons. Then she gave me a hug.

Liquidating Perry

I accosted a doctor roving about the ICU. It's about my dad, I said. I meant to say 'Perry.' 'Dad' just slipped out.
    What's next? I asked her.
    She didn't respond. There was no next.

Liquidating Perry

I found Perry's debit card in his wallet, which had been stowed away in a duffel bag with some medication and (a treat, I suppose, for when he finished radiation) an unopened pack of menthol cigarettes.
0100.
I withdrew what little money he had, $60. I didn't know what I would need it for. But I didn't want the bank to have it.

Liquidating Perry

The next night Perry was moved out of intensive care and into hospice. I wasn't there to see him transported out; it wasn't a ride I was invited along. He was quite tired. I imagine he woke up and tried joking with the ambulance crew.

Within hours of arriving at hospice Perry slipped into a morphine coma. His room was bare bones. No cords, a respirator, a call button. That's it. He was wrapped in his bedclothes like a papoose. Someone had mercifully muted the television, on *Let's Make a Deal*.

When we die, Monty Hall will show us what's behind Door #1.

Two hours before he died a nurse came in, apologized, and said Perry was taking his last breaths.

Which, she added, could last for hours.

I held Perry by the forearm. I tried to will him to stop breathing.

I believe he was too embarrassed to expire in front of me.

His lips were quivering but there was no sound. He could have been trying to speak to Leo or Eloise. I was told, toward the end, to accept unseen people in the room as real.

An hour before he died, a social worker came in, apologized, and asked if I had made any burial arrangements.

I hadn't.

She assured me that she'd give me a discount if I used her family's mortuary.

Forty-five minutes before he died my wife called and asked if I could pick up her uncle from the airport, a half-hour away.

Perry was firm to the touch. His flesh had hardened. He looked thin but not near death. His elbow didn't feel dead. His lungs were laboring but fighting. It was like there was a megaphone on his breathing. They were deep, laborious heaves.

Liquidating Perry

    I told myself that a deceased Perry wasn't the Perry he'd want me to see. I convinced myself that I had too big of a life, that my life wasn't confined to his death.
    I'm giving you fifteen minutes, I told him. Please. Don't hold on. I can't wait here. I won't.
    I gave him twenty. I kissed his forehead and drove away.
    He died while I was at the Baggage Claim, Palm Springs Int'l. Terminal Two.

Liquidating Perry

We cling, all of us, like lint to the broom of life.

Perry owed us nothing. He did not even owe us his old age.

It really wasn't a terrible day, just a lot of bad news, all at once. It was over. I could breathe.

He is now where the clouds don't get any higher, in the gridlock and polyglut of souls.

I should not have told him he was dying. He folded his hand awfully fast.

That night I flew home to San Francisco, where the flags were flying at half-staff, but not for him. When the pastor at the Rescue Mission telephoned the next day with his condolences and with every faith that Perry had, at the millisecond after his death, touched the face of Jesus, and was in heaven and no longer in pain, I was too touched by the gesture to say that Perry first had a layover in Phoenix, where his bodily vitals were being parted out for medical research.

Chapter Seven – Patrón Saint

Obituaries are embellishments. They are not to be read carelessly. After college I worked on the obit desk for a wire service. I wrote Gerald Ford's, for example, six months before he died. This is the privilege of public figures. As for the rest of us … we hope there's a strong pen in the family.

Obituaries are existential. The when and where and what trump the how and why. "Old age" is an insufficient cause of death. Case in point:

"Perry Steven Amendt died from renal failure on November 6th, 2012, in Palm Desert, CA. He was 59."

Obituaries are ineffable. Occasionally I would be permitted to insert radical things, like the color of the deceased's eyes.

I was trained to synthesize life in ten column inches. I avoided adjectives, descriptors. Any survivors were strangers to me.

Until I was one.

Liquidating Perry

Condolences are either too much or not enough. I almost wanted to step in and interrupt before they were offered. I only wanted to hear 'I'm sorry,' but you'd be surprised how few people offered even that.

The closure was for Perry, it seemed, and not for them.

There were the requisite condolences I received from his siblings.

My uncle, who did not speak to Perry for twenty years, wrote me this:

Wanted to let you know how sorry we are about your Dad's passing.

I haven't heard from him since.

My grandmother, Kathleen's mom, was a little more expansive.

Sorry to hear about your dad. I know a little about losing one's parent. Even when I've been prepared for the event, and thought it would be the best thing that could happen for the person suffering, there is an unexplainable pain and a sense of loss that I can't put into words. I keep trying to write my thoughts, but I truly can't put them into words. There simply aren't any. Just know that I'm feeling for you and with you and I'm sorry.

Oh the folly of trying to figure all things out, and of trying to understand the incomprehensible, but we would like to have the answers. Bad genes? No. Bad environment? No. Who knows? Looking back at Kathleen it is hard for me to see her as she once was. It certainly wasn't either you or Travis. I could read through a little of your pain as you related the last events of your dad's life. You might guess that, to you, I have an oversimplification of the ills of this world, and it's Biblical. An enemy has done this. And it's not going to get better.

Yes, your mother is still in Springfield. I only hear from her if she needs something desperately. It's sad that she gets herself in these desperate situations, but then I'm (can't say I'm happy) fortunate that

I can help, and that through these situations I can know she's still alive, if one can call her lifestyle living.

And this, from my aunt Aleta:

You might want to know about a phone call I received right after Perry passed. It was from his Radiologist (I've lost his name). He called to tell me what a wonderful person Perry was. He said he always had a positive attitude and was more than a patient; he was a friend. He said he could not sleep at night if he did not call me. My phone number was the only one he had. This doctor said Perry was always on time for his appointments and was smiling. He knew something was wrong when he did not come to his normal Friday appointment. He had nothing but good to say.

Liquidating Perry

Perry is not like Jean Simmons, who existed so much on film, visually, that nothing need exist of her on paper. There is no home movie of him, no VHS of him, no PSA as there should have been. Nor did we communicate by voicemail, until a few weeks before he died, when he detailed his progress, and after he died I realized this was the only voice I had of him. One afternoon while I was on my lunch break on San Francisco's Market Street, I fumbled and shattered my mobile phone. I hope there weren't any voicemails you wanted to save, my technician said. I shook my head. There weren't. It was time to delete.

Maturation doesn't happen overnight. You learn what to look back on, to look back on the right things. Still, I'm wary of meditating on me. It's why I don't run or jog often – all I can think about is breathing, and my breath is not compelling.

What I remember more than Perry's voice was his laugh. It was more of a wry smile, an a-ha, a snicker. He guffawed when he laughed. He often snorted.

Liquidating Perry

When Perry was no longer, I did not get the full reality, rather, the gravity, of what had just happened. I was relieved and all I could see was my relief. Two weeks later it was Thanksgiving and I'm still ashamed of how I treated my in-laws, surly, shut-off.

It's the first holiday that's hardest when you lose a parent.

Most parents leave you something. Perry left me this. He is my inheritance.

It was not indecent of him not to leave behind an insurance policy. Like Eloise, he'd have lied on it somewhere.

The day after Thanksgiving a friend of Perry's called me out-of-the-blue. He had some stuff of Perry's, probably invaluable to me.

I didn't call him back. He stopped calling.

I have what Perry had at the Mission. I have his notes on apartment hunting, his medical journal.

It's the plans of a dying man. I think his vision of his future was never more vivid.

The journal indicates where he received treatment, when and from whom.

I don't know if it was for him, or for me.

Liquidating Perry

That December, Perry's remains arrived via FedEx, with a note attached:
Your special package.
On the death certificate some clerk had left the second 'r' out of San Bernardino, one of Perry's pet peeves.

I swore I wouldn't keep him in the closet. I thought he should be where he had never visited, and always wanted to: the Missions north of Santa Barbara.

He was fascinated by California history. California was mostly his religion.

On a Saturday morning in January 2013 my wife and I buckled Perry up and went.

As I write this Father Junipero Serra, the man who founded the Missions, all 23 of them from San Diego to Sonoma, is up for sainthood.

I'm not worried about canonizing Perry, but lionizing him.

Sonoma's Mission – an hour's drive from San Francisco – is the youngest of all of them, and also the northernmost. As we stalked for parking spots I realized I had no way of smuggling Perry inside. His urn was conspicuously urn-like.

Fortunately, we had stopped at Starbucks along the way.

I dried out one of the to-go cups and dunked it in the urn until I had about a fifth of Perry.

A fifth. Perry's favorite measurement.

Inside the Mission foyer a uniformed docent stopped me.

No liquids allowed inside, he said.

You don't want to see him without his coffee, my wife said.

But drinks were allowed in the courtyard, small and crowded and I wasn't sure where to pour Perry out. The cactus garden looked too prickly and the kiln was out because I didn't want him incinerated twice.

Liquidating Perry

  I found a tree in a back corner that looked good enough.
  I removed the lid. A latte, I think it had been. Perry's ashes sort of burped out. My wife chastised me.
  You could have tried to sprinkle him, she said.
  They don't teach any of this. There is no finishing school for men. There is no graceful way.

After Sonoma, we headed south. At Mission Soledad I dumped him into an archaeological excavation as the workers were out to lunch. At Mission San Miguel I almost took a sip from the wrong Starbucks cup.

Along the 101, as I drove, I contemplated pulling over and stealing one of the hundreds of El Camino Real bells that commemorate this part of the state's history, the Catholic part, the dreadful peonage part.

Our final stop on the Perry roadshow was the Mission Santa Barbara, very early in the morning, near daybreak. It could have been my reluctance to part with Perry, but for the life of me I couldn't find a spot that was appropriate to dump him.

We noticed a Stations of the Cross off to the side, with a good view of the Pacific Ocean, amidst a well-manicured grove of olive trees.

The Olive Garden.

He loved California. He also loved breadsticks.

Perry was fine in my fingers. The last of him fell out like quicksand. We laughed and cried and threw out the urn, and like John Wayne, drove off into the sunrise.

Liquidating Perry

Two years after his death I received my fourth condolence letter.

Dear Zachary Amendt,

We are deeply sorry for your loss. We have reviewed your request to obtain the contents of account, perryamendt@gmail.com, and accompanying documentation. In order to proceed, we require a U.S. Court Order, directed to Google Inc. and which specify the following:

That the decedent is deceased;
That the decedent is the sole account holder of the named account;
That the requesting party has a legal right to obtain the content;
Disclosure of the content would not violate any applicable laws, including but not limited to the Electronic Communications Privacy Act and any state equivalent;
The specific Gmail content being requested;
That Google Inc. is ordered to produce the requested Gmail content to requesting party and the location to which production needs to be made;
That requesting party must attach the order to an email sent to postmortemrequests@google.com.

Best regards,

The Google Team

The modern biographer need only know his subject's passwords, then cut and paste.

This was one of those instances where Perry's password was stronger than my strongest conjecture.

Liquidating Perry

Double rainbows and unicorns. For some people that's life. For some people, life is Disneyland.

Fate is not cruel. Endings don't have to be merciful. I found in Perry's effects from the Rescue Mission a story of his from a creative writing course at Aquinas – he was 17 then – which he titled 'My Dad' (*"Not at all flashy or extremely original, but still fine,"* his teacher had written. "A-.") I also found a short story of his I didn't know existed.

Our juvenilia belongs in Juvenile Hall. Perry's 'In Peril of Death' is five pages long and fairly terrible. But as it's the clever thefts that perpetuate the culture and give it texture – jazz musicians have been cribbing melodies for almost a full century longer than rappers have been pirating beats – when asked to give a reading after his death I thought it was appropriate to go the Nat King and Natalie Cole route, the 'Unforgettable' route, and re-write every other sentence of his 'Peril.'

What I always wanted, I think, was a duet with Perry.

IN PERIL OF DEATH

Bill Gunther was not an easy man to scare. But he had an aversion to crowds and didn't understand things like Coachella, or Woodstock, or people. In other words, Bill Gunther was a rough man – rough in the sense of rough and tumble, rough riders, beef jerky.

Bill was over the Amazon River in a small commercial airplane with two passengers and no fuel. He was a bush pilot, calm under stress, no biggie. He was en route to Rio de Janerio on a gig for Brazil Airways. It was a good job even though it meant a lot of sitting and logs and navigating by sextant which he never really learned how to use.

The plane was sluggish, unresponsive. Gunther had to find a place to land the plane, and in a hurry! It occurred to him, as he set the nose down, that he was wary of heights as a child, that if he had grounded himself then he would never have to descend, not ever. He had a sweet tooth, an affinity for chocolate and westerns. Life on land was a level life, one horizon. The stars were less fickle. The wheels were always down.

Gunther spotted a small clearing in the dense trees of the jungle. The plan hit the ground with a tremendous jolt that ripped off the wings completely and sent the plane sliding through the underbrush of the clearing and into a maze of trees.

Miraculously, neither Gunther nor his passengers was badly injured.

However, they had no guns, knives, or food.

With his general knowledge of his whereabouts, Gunther figured in what general direction they would go. One of his passengers, Dr. Henry, had broken his femur during the crash, and while he was ambulatory, with a makeshift splint, it was likely that if Gunther judged wrong, at least one passenger would not make it.

The three men started off, physically strong, materially weak, and mentally only hopeful and optimistic.

By nightfall they had made very good progress. The forest growth was reasonably thin. That night they stayed in a cave they fashioned out of bamboo and mud. At sunrise they continued their journey. After an hour or so it began to rain, to monsoon. Gunther didn't expect rain this sudden and thick. His visibility was no more than twenty yards. In just a half-day they were beginning to show signs of exhaustion, especially Dr. Henry, whose injury was becoming gangrenous. Three times Henry had to stop and rest. Each time the rest was longer. This is exactly what Gunther was afraid would happen. They had not yet journeyed more than three days and not covered more than eight miles.

If they were not going in the right direction, they had two chances of survival: very slim and none at all.

At sunrise Gunther left, on his own. The raining had not ceased for even a second, but Gunther didn't stop. He couldn't stop. He came to a ravine which the torrential rains had turned into a small river. He planted his foot on a large rock. It gave way. When he came to he found himself half-submerged in water, and he could see bone emerging from the skin just below his ankle. He must go on! Gunther was totally exhausted and delirious with pain. On he crawled. He was numb without any sense of time or direction. On he went for three days, four, five. He had no feeling of hunger or thirst. He crawled on and on. He had lost hope! Why he continued on he didn't know.

Suddenly he could go no farther. He propped himself against a log. He thought. He had been a quiet, timid child. His grandfather had been in the Air Corps, a bombardier. He had been weaned on stories of valor, lies. The end was inconceivable and it had always been

Liquidating Perry

Gunther's idea – a reckoning, a conjecture – that it was impossible for life to end in anything but more life.

He always knew what his 'rosebud' would be, his last words. Only he imagined someone somewhere would take note of it. So he yelled. He yelled as loud as he could for what seemed like an eternity. No one answered. He yelled louder, still louder, but no-one came.

And had you been a native of the Amazon that day, within earshot, you'd have wondered who it was, what beast or bird, shouting 'Ovaltine' 'Ovaltine', in a strong but diminishing, and eventually dim, voice.

Liquidating Perry

The world is relatively small, relative to the limits of our imaginations. Our imagination can drain the ocean. It can fathom more fathoms.

These words don't always go where I wanted them to, or where they should. This is a mash-up of Perry and me. Sometimes I don't know where he ends and I begin. It's not just what I think about him – it's what he was and what I am and what we jointly are. I hope to forget not Perry but the absence of Perry, and if this exists then he exists. He is a matter of public record. He is in the annals like he always wanted to be.

Our ephemeral gifts dissipate, but like a stock or commodity that's plummeting, we can't lose all of the value of our gift: a remnant always remains. As with Perry. I save face for him, in the places he was unable to. I like to picture him at 24, robust, thirsty, debonair, insouciant, waiting after work to meet a girl who he knows will not show.

Leaning against the bar. Waiting to wait.

Liquidating Perry

ABOUT THE AUTHOR

Zachary Amendt's short fiction has appeared in anthologies alongside George Saunders, James Brown and Jonathan Ames. He is the author of the story collection STAY (Montag Press Collective, 2014).

Liquidating Perry

Made in the USA
San Bernardino, CA
07 May 2016